Lesley Ch

My 50th Birthday Bucket List and other Ramblings

A year (and a bit) of 50 memorable experiences

For Josh

*To Lauren
with love & sparkles
from
Lesley x*

Copyright © Lesley Charlton (2019)

The right of Lesley Charlton to be identified as author of this work has been asserted by her in accordance with section 77 and 78 of the Copyright, Designs and Patents Act 1988.

All rights reserved. No part of this publication may be reproduced, stored in a retrieval system, or transmitted in any form or by any means, electronic, mechanical, photocopying, recording or otherwise, without the prior permission of the publishers.

Any person who commits any unauthorised act in relation to the publication may be liable to criminal prosecution and civil claims for damages.

A CIP catalogue record for this title is available from the British Library.

ISBN 978-1-9162574-0-5 (Paperback)
ISBN 978-1-9162574-1-2 (ePub e-book)

First Published 2019 by Love and Sparkles Publishing

As much of this book recognises how fortunate I have been with my life's travels, the sale of each copy will supply a donation to the Travel Foundation, supporting tourism that benefits local people and protects the environment.

My 50th Birthday Bucket List and other Ramblings
A year (and a bit) of 50 memorable experiences

by
Lesley Charlton

A story about me. Written primarily for my own benefit, to look back on in years to come but out there in case anyone else would like to read have a read and perhaps be inspired to make a Bucket List of their own.

Dedicated to my Dad
Leslie William Harris
(14th March 1926 - 19th November 2017)

Sadly, Dad didn't live long enough to read this book but luckily he was still around to enjoy following my exploits, listening to my stories and seeing my photos from this memorable year.

I am eternally grateful for the wanderlust I inherited from him, his unwavering support and the courage he instilled in me to follow my dreams. Thanks Dad.

with love and sparkles

Contents

Introduction 5

Chapter 1 Start a Bucket List Blog 14

Chapter 2 Contact someone with your own name ... 20

Chapter 3 Make a snow angel 23

Chapter 4 Finish your 40th Birthday photo album . 25

Chapter 5 Make a basket 31

Chapter 6 Sleep in a lighthouse 41

Chapters 7 & 8 Visit Marrakech and go White Water Rafting in the High Atlas Mountains & Sleep under the stars 45

Chapter 9 Serve food at a soup kitchen 68

Chapter 10 Plan celebrations for Josh's 18th and my 50th Birthdays 75

Chapter 11 Kayak from Christchurch to Ringwood 79

Chapter 12 Go to the Isle of Wight Festival 87

Chapter 13 Attend the Summer Solstice at Stonehenge 94

Chapters 14 & 15 Visit 50 pubs in Gosport (past and present) & Own an original piece of Art 98

Chapters 16 & 17 Take part in a Run or Dye event & Change the colour of your hair 105

Chapter 18 Pack your bags and set off with no fixed agenda 109

Chapter 19 Get a log burner installed 115

Chapter 20	Get Maizie Restored	117
Chapter 21	Go to the Sidmouth Folk Festival	127
Chapter 22	Have a "Girls' Night In"	139
Chapter 23	Take part in a Murder Mystery	144
Chapter 24	Visit Buckingham Palace	150
Chapter 25	Go Clubbing in Ibiza	153
Chapter 26	Ride the longest zip line in Europe	159
Chapter 27	Go on a Kayak Safari in Cornwall	166
Chapters 28 & 29	Cycle the Camel Trail & Ride a tandem	172
Chapter 30	The "Pembrokeshire Surprise"	182
Chapter 31	Visit Venice	189
Chapter 32	Go to the Opera	197
Chapter 33	Complete the Monopoly Board Challenge	201
Chapter 34	Buy something at an auction	204
Chapter 35	Walk to Winchester *(from home!)*	209
Chapter 36	Send a message in a bottle	211
Chapter 37	Go on a ghost walk	213
Chapter 38	Take a trip on the Eurostar	216
Chapter 39	Plan someone else's 50th Birthday	222
Chapter 40	Visit Lumiere London	237
Chapter 41	Retire at Fifty	242
Chapter 42	Attend the Adventure Travel Show	250

Chapter 43 Take part in Fawlty Towers - The Dining Experience 255

Chapters 44 & 45 Visit Pompeii & Vesuvius 257

Chapter 46 Visit the Sky Garden 264

Chapter 47 Celebrate Dad's 90th Birthday 270

Chapter 48 Make a personalised blanket.............. 276

Chapter 49 Complete a project with crocheted flowers 278

Chapter 50 Write a book about my 50th Birthday Bucket List... 281

Introduction

In the beginning were the two words ... "Bucket" and "List". Haven't you always wanted to do a Bucket List? I know I have. In some ways, my whole life has been a bit of a Bucket List, which I thought I should commit to print, in the hope that my gorgeous son, Josh, might think his Mum wasn't so bad after all. Not that I'm anything special. I guess I'm clever enough but I've never been good at anything in particular, always preferring to "have a go" at lots of different things, rather than specialising in anything specific. I've always been more of a people person than an academic or career-driven person. I've been adventurous, within my own boundaries but I know my limitations. I love making friends and having experiences but I'm not an out and out adventurer. I just like pushing myself ... a little bit.

When I was eleven, living in Somerset, a Parachute Display Team dropped into a fete in Crewkerne and I said to my parents "One day I'm going to do that" to which my Mum's response was "Over my dead body!" Luckily, despite her statement, she lived to see me fulfil that ambition, when at the age of eighteen, at the Royal Naval and Royal Marine Sport Parachute Association at Dunkeswell in Devon, I turned my dream into reality. In fact, it was at Dunkeswell that I met Josh's Dad Steve, my late husband, although how we met is a story for another day ... or maybe another book!

I did my static line course, in the days before tandem jumps and AFF (Accelerated Free Fall) were even an option and became a licensed free fall skydiver. When I was learning, before you progressed to the sleek ram-air square parachutes that we recognise today, you had to practice your skills on something far less sophisticated. For your static line jumps, when you were still attached to the plane and your parachute opened automatically on exit, you would use aero conical chutes which had very basic manoeuvrability. Early free fall jumps were carried out using old T-10 chutes, which were designed in the 1950s and had equally basic controls, i.e. pull on the left riser (strap) to turn left, the right riser to turn right and if you had the strength, you could pull on both risers simultaneously to dump air out of the back of the chute and lose height. Both of these "rounds" required the use of a very unattractive and cumbersome belly mounted reserve chute which, when worn together, made you look a little like a pregnant Hunchback of Notre Dame. How things have progressed!

From being a DZ Doris ("DZ" - the Drop Zone of a skydiving centre and "Doris" - the generic name given to all young ladies on a DZ!) I moved on to be air/ground crew and general dog's body, i.e. commentary, PR and pyrotechnic operative (I let off the flares!), for the Royal Navy Parachute Display Team known as the "Raiders". They used to entertain at events such as Military Open Days, Navy Days in Portsmouth Dockyard and the annual tri-nation Allied Forces Day Parade in Berlin (before the wall came down).

I loved accompanying the British Team to Berlin and feel very privileged to have had the opportunity to take part in activities that were, generally, not available to civilian personnel, although getting arrested at Checkpoint Charlie one year hadn't been on the agenda (obviously). As dependants of Serving Personnel, we were able to cross the border under the military umbrella and as such, were deemed "untouchable" by the border guards. However, this particular year, just before we'd arrived, there had been a successful escape from East Germany. A young man had hidden his girlfriend in the hollowed-out front seat of his mini, which was now on prominent display on the Western side of the checkpoint. Whenever an escape such as this succeeded, the border guards were reprimanded and subsequently on high alert, in an endeavour to arrest somebody from the West, in retribution.

Unaware of this, four of us; Bob, his wife Karon, Steve and myself, set off across the border, through the military channel as usual. However, on this occasion, Karon and I, who were obviously not in uniform, were politely separated from our husbands who, as per the regulations, were in uniform. We were ushered down a separate channel and once we were out of sight of the military crossing, the mood of the guards changed. We were escorted, at gunpoint, into a chained-off holding area, where different officers would take it in turn to come and shout aggressively at us in German. Although they didn't actually touch us, they would get so close that you could feel their breath on your face as they barked their demands, not that we knew what their demands were as neither of us spoke German. They took our passports and all our cash which, due to the exchange rate of four East German Marks to every one West German Mark (a provocative attempt to demonstrate superiority I believe), was perceived as quite a substantial amount that side of the Iron Curtain. As other civilians passed by, we tried asking them to translate for us, or to let our husbands know what was happening to us, once they'd crossed the border. However they too would be threatened at gunpoint and were therefore, quite understandably, too afraid to talk to us. We kept having documents thrust at us to sign but as we had no idea what they said, we refused. To make matters even more tricky, Karon was pregnant. We tried to convey this to our captors but they completely ignored the situation, refusing to even allow her a glass of water. Becoming increasingly concerned for her welfare, we decided the only thing to do was to comply with their demands, in an attempt to get out of there. When the next stern-faced guard appeared, with an even longer form for us to sign, we consented. A short time later, a smiling guard appeared, handed us back our passports, together with a copy of the forms we'd signed, then removed the chain boundary and indicated that we were free to go, wishing us a nice day in perfect English!

Rather shaken, we were reunited with Bob and Steve on the Eastern side. They had been in such a quandary. Rules dictated that Military Personnel were never to be alone in the East, which meant it was impossible to have one of them on each side of the border to wait for us. They had no idea what was going on, or if we would be sent back to the West or allowed to cross to the East. Other civilians passing through were forbidden to talk to them and the border guards on the military channel refused to get involved … and of course, these were the days WELL before mobile phones. They didn't want to cross back to the West in case we arrived in the East and they weren't there. This would leave us in a very vulnerable situation, without the military protection offered to us when we were accompanying them, so all they could do was wait and what an unimaginably agonising wait it was. It had been distressing for us but it must have been unbearable for them. After a brief explanation of what we had encountered, the boys decided we should cross straight back to the West. The border guards, again in English, sarcastically commented on our brief stay and said that they hoped we'd had a nice visit.

Once safely back in the West, we reported the incident to the appropriate people and later that afternoon, we received a visit from a British gentleman who, rather bizarrely, resembled Herr Flick of the Gestapo, from the British sitcom 'Allo 'Allo!, complete with gold, round-rimmed glasses and full-length leather coat (although without the limp). He gave us a thorough debrief and casually stated that we were lucky to have got away with just a three-hour ordeal, as normally we would have been detained for twenty-four hours and strip searched! We asked him to translate the forms we'd signed and apparently, we'd admitted to smuggling currency into the East and subsequently received a court summons. I remember asking him what would happen to us when we appeared at our trial, to which he laughed, saying we would not, of course, be attending as the summons was not recognised in the West. However, if we were to cross into the East again, we would most likely be arrested!!! Needless to say, we never crossed again. As scary as it was at the time, it's a great story to tell now and what an experience!

I had other exhilarating escapades during our trips to Berlin. I worked with the French Foreign Legion where, during practice jumps for the Parade, I was invited onto the flight deck of their Hercules C-130 aircraft, where the only thing you see on the ascent, after take-off, is blue skies and the only thing you see on the descent, before landing, is the ground. What a magnificent aircraft that was. With the American forces, I was allowed to lean out of the side-opening doors of their Apache helicopters as we flew along the Berlin wall, skimming tantalisingly (and presumably intentionally provokingly, as we were still in the midst of the Cold War) close to the edge of no-man's land, just a few hundred feet above the ground. Treasured memories of exciting times before the health and safety restrictions of today and in an era when red tape was a little more flexible, "allowing" a civilian like me to take part in such antics.

But let's return to my introduction. These days I think I'm pretty comfortable in my own skin. Generally, I've nothing to prove to anybody apart from myself and even that I don't take too seriously but if I believe something might be fun, or a bit of a challenge, I tend to think, "Why not?" As the age old saying goes … you only live once and as one of the significant men in my life sadly never made his half century, it seemed only right to celebrate that fact that I did by making a Bucket List of things to achieve in my fiftieth year.

Of course, as with all things in life, nothing ever goes exactly to plan, so there is a little poetic licence here. Like the fact that I have extended my "year", starting in January 2015 and finishing ... well, now really. And the fact that my Bucket List evolved from the original one as the year progressed ... but those are mere details.

So here I sit, in one of my favourite boltholes - Costa Teguise, Lanzarote, writing a book about this phase of my life. I say one of my favourite boltholes but probably my absolute favourite is Kitzbühel, Austria, with one of my besties Aly, who has picked me up, dusted me down and sent me back out there on many occasions. Aly's is where I went for my fortieth Birthday, where she served me breakfast on her balcony, in the snow, then sent me Paragliding seventeen-hundred metres above sea level, from the top of the Hahnenkamm. Again, a story for another day (or another tome). I will attempt not to digress from the stories intended for this book too much but as my friends will testify, there always seems to be a tale to tell and I'm always more than happy to tell it, so staying on track may prove tricky ... but I'll try.

Back to where I am now. Sitting at my makeshift desk in Lanzarote, listening to my music, collating the evidence, trying to decide how to document the ins and outs of the "year" into something resembling the form of a book. I say listening to my music but these days, despite studying Computer Science at A Level, I'm a bit of a technophobe, leaving all that wizardry to my techie husband, KC The Gadget Man ... aka Mr C. What he doesn't know about technology isn't worth knowing, hence I don't bother. So, I set off on this mission with all the iGadgets I could fit in my hand luggage but I forgot to ask him to sort out the music before I left. My mobile has an eclectic mix of running songs, for the gym (not great for reflective writing) so I am resorting to the music on my laptop, which is limited, due to the lack of space because of the many, many photos I insisted on putting on here. In the background I have the folk tunes of one of the other men in my life - Mike Rosenberg, aka Passenger (who I invited to do a House Gig at ours once but you can find out about that later), interspersed with a selection of melodies from the album Café Morocco! I have no idea why that is on my laptop as, when we went to Morocco, we had no technology with us whatsoever but now I'm jumping ahead again, you'll need to read on to find out more about that one too.

So, I'm in a location chosen to enable me to concentrate, with "interesting" music in the background, deciding on the best way to catalogue my adventures, finally choosing to work through in date order. I keep an online diary, take loads of photos and have dabbled with being a Blogger (I had a few followers when we got married in Borneo and climbed Mount Kinabalu), so I have plenty of material and this will form the framework for my book. Rather than one long story, I have decided to write in chronological order, in a diary format, for each of the fifty things on my List but I think I should start with how it all began.

By the first day of January 2015, I wanted to have a list in place, of fifty things to achieve in my fiftieth year. I had lots of ideas of my own and a few from friends who wanted to contribute or make suggestions. I used these, padded out with ideas from other people's lists that I'd Googled ... well, what else does one do these days?!?

My final List doesn't differ hugely from the original and is a combination of things that I love, things I haven't done before, things I can keep and things my friends think I should do! All in all, I think I had quite an amazing year. I'd like to thank in advance everyone who has taken part and my ever-tolerant husband for tagging along with me ... most of the time!

Chapter One

(1st January 2015)

Start a Bucket List Blog

After a hectic New Year's Eve party at ours, once the guests had left and the clearing up had been done, it was a Duvet Day and time to make a start on "the List". I had pondered for a long time about how to approach it and the parameters I would be working within. I decided that, rather than starting on my fiftieth birthday, I would start at the beginning of the calendar year, with the proviso that I could extend to my fifty-first birthday if I needed a little extra time. Little did I know, the final chapter would be extended even further! I already had some ideas but now was the time to pull it all together and start my Blog, so people could engage in the shenanigans, if they chose to. As mentioned, I've enjoyed creating Blogs for specific events and adventures over the years, so I knew how to set one up and began creating fifty entries from my initial draft.

As I said, I'd poached some entries from other people, as I really wanted to have fifty "things" right from the get-go, rather than forty-odd "things" and some blank spaces. As I progressed through the year, some of these were replaced with more bespoke objectives. Some of my early ideas could not be completed for one reason or another. For example, staying on Brownsea Island, which was possible when I started my Blog, as Mr C was working part-time at Waitrose and as a John Lewis Partner, we had access to this. However, when he handed in his notice, to concentrate on developing his own business, we had to cancel, or should I say they cancelled us, as we were no longer entitled to this perk. I also wanted to go diving in Swanage but every time we planned to go, the weather or diving conditions were against us and in the end, we just ran out of time. The Dive Centre only operates from May to October and we'd have had to do it through them as, being "resort divers" and usually diving in much warmer, sunnier climes, we don't have our own kit, so need to hire it. Having said that, I did manage to finally tick that box (the dive, not the kit ownership) … in my fifty-third year!

We have a bit of an affiliation with Swanage and if the weather is looking good and we have a spare day or two, which isn't often, we jump into Ruby, our beloved VW campervan, who is always prepped and ready to go, head to the Sandbanks Ferry, cross to Studland and then onwards, to our favourite wild camping spot on the Jurassic Coast, where we have awesome camp fires under the stars and meet some great, like-minded people. On our way home, we often drop into Swanage and buy a ticket to promenade along the restored Victorian pier. You can Sponsor a Plank, to assist with restoration work. You do this by buying a brass plaque, as we did for our anniversary a couple of years ago, which is then secured to one of the restored planks on the pier. If you ever visit, check it out and give it a polish for us - number 9469 on Row H. You can borrow a little cloth bag containing rags and a tin of Brasso from the ticket office. Our plaque reads *"Love and Sparkles for KC The Gadget Man"*, which was a perfect description of our life at that time.

The story behind this wording, in case you were wondering, is that when Mr C took voluntary redundancy, a few years ago, we embraced it as an opportunity rather than a disaster. I was working as a Schools Liaison Officer part-time … very part-time … in fact it was just one day a week … oh and term time only … but it was a proper job and I took it very seriously - honestly! Anyway, I was out doing a school visit in Petersfield one wet and windy day and took Mr C along for the ride, as he was on gardening leave. He sat in the car and read his book, while I did my presentation in the school then, when I'd finished, we went into town for a coffee, to talk about what our skill sets were and if we could think of something we could "do" together.

We wandered into the old Woolworths store, which was now one of the pound shops, looking for inspiration (yes, seriously!). I've always been creative, whereas Mr C, as I said before, enjoys science and technology. We chatted as we wandered up and down the aisles, thinking of something we could perhaps make and sell. I was looking at the arts and crafts, thinking about how I could package "it", whatever "it" was going to be and he was looking at "things", that people might actually buy. It would have to be something reasonably cheap to make but that people could actually use. We pondered some very silly ideas … and then we came up with, what we thought was, a brilliant one. Some years ago, we'd seen some pinecones that create wonderful coloured flames when you burn them. Pinecones are cheap (well, free actually if you gather them yourself), Mr C was confident that he knew enough about chemistry to come up with a magic formula and I was confident that I could package them, to make them look attractive. Bingo! Right there and then we knew exactly what the name for our aspiring business would be - Love and Sparkles. It was the way I always signed off my messages and kind of fitted the "corporate image" we envisaged.

The next few months were filled with pinecone gathering, sometimes collecting twenty kilos at a time … each! It was autumn and if it had been a stormy, windy night, we'd be out around the country parks with our garden recycle bags, "harvesting". We'd even have competitions as to who could collect the most on each trip. Armed with our heavy-duty sacks, we would be fiercely protective if we found an area that delivered the mother-load, staking our claim with phrases like "I found it first". Returning to the car, we would use our portable digital luggage scales to determine the winner, often much to the amusement of any other people in the car park. Ah, those halcyon days. Mr C ordered all sorts of chemicals, which he would experiment with and refine, whilst testing the best way to actually process the pinecones, to achieve the results we were looking for. At night, we would be out in the back garden, trying each new creation out in our old chimenea, until he perfected the recipe. At this point, I think Pyrotechnics R Us would have been a more fitting business title. In the meantime, I spent hours designing and making pretty boxes and labels. Our house was a production line of commodities and packaging with wrappings, cones and chemicals everywhere. A cross between Pinterest and Breaking Bad!

Our "retail outlets" were various fetes and craft markets, so when we weren't making, we were selling ... except we weren't really selling. Sometimes we didn't even make enough to cover the cost of our pitch! We diversified into various other things made with pinecones and/or wax ... firelighters, hanging ornaments, teacup candles. We had lots of fun but it was never going to make us any real money. When we look back, we have never worked so hard, for so many hours a day and had so much fun but it soon became obvious that Love and Sparkles was only ever going to be a hobby and not a business. So, it was back to the drawing board.

Sitting in the hot tub one afternoon, we went back to basics. Blank canvas - what did Mr C enjoy? The answer was staring us in the face ... gadgets! To be honest, what man doesn't like a gadget? Except he loved them and more importantly, he knew all about them. He was always fixing things for friends and family, sorting out their computers and their mobile phones, keeping up to date with technology and showing people how to use it (except his wife of course ... that would be grounds for divorce!!!). Of course, there were questions. Would there be a market for it? Would people pay for services like that? The short answer to both of those questions is "Yes" and that is how KC The Gadget Man was born. Far more lucrative than Love and Sparkles and far less messy at home. So, when thinking of an inscription for our anniversary plaque, "Love and Sparkles for KC The Gadget Man" was the obvious choice, commemorating our transition from "living to work" to "working to live", which has given us the flexibility to do what we want, when we want (pretty much) and fulfil some of these madcap ideas that are my Bucket List … and more! You see, I've digressed again. I said I would. Right, let's get back on track and return to the Blog.

As it happens, although I started my Blog with great gusto, it didn't evolve quite as I'd planned. Originally, it was going to be a way for my friends to follow my exploits and make their comments and suggestions along the way. Bizarrely, in this day and age, I reverted to a paper version for this task! In our hallway we have a huge map of the world, which we cover with sticky dots, denoting; where we have been, where we have dived and where we would like to go on our never-ending wish list of travel. Surrounding the map is a framed photograph of each of the countries we have visited. People always pause to look at it, it's a great conversation piece, which often prompted the question "How's the Bucket List going?". So, I decided to print the List on paper and stick it on the wall, next to the map, ticking off the things that had been achieved and showing the things that were planned. Placing it here also meant people could write on it. Amazingly, nobody wrote anything inappropriate … which shows they are all much more mature than me, as I think the temptation to do so would have been far too great if I was in their shoes. So, although my Blog didn't pan out as I'd envisaged, I'm still going to claim this as an achievement and tick it off my List because I did "start" one and it did provide the substructure I was looking for.

Chapter Two

(6th January 2015)

Contact someone with your own name

OK, so I confess, this is an idea I stole from someone else's Bucket List on the internet but it seemed like a fun thing to do and when I started, I had no idea just how successful it would be. Of course, in this day and age, the obvious place to start is Facebook. I typed in Lesley Charlton and came up with seven possibilities. I looked at the thumbnail profile pictures for each and one was absolutely perfect. This is the message I sent with my Friend Request;

Hi Lesley
One of the things on my 50th Birthday Bucket List is to contact another Lesley Charlton so I wondered if you would like to be my Facebook Friend and if you are happy to appear on my 50th Birthday Bucket List Blog as an achievement? No worries if you'd rather not but I chose you from all the Lesley Charltons on Facebook as you have hair like mine!
Best wishes
Lesley (Charlton)

How excited was I when my Timeline pinged "Became friends with Lesley Charlton on Facebook"! Of course, now she was my friend, I could find out more about her, which is a bit creepy I know but I'm sure we've all done a bit of Facebook stalking and this was, after all, in the name of research as, one day, I would be writing a book (see Chapter 50 ... or just carry on reading!!!). The thing that struck me first was that, although she had not listed where she lived, she had checked in (Facebook speak) to a restaurant, very close to a village where I had once lived in Somerset, so I just HAD to ask the question;

Me: *Can I be cheeky and ask which area you live in? Not stalking you* **(I lied)**, *just interested!*
Lesley: *Somerset.*
Me: *Oh my! I lived in North Perrott and Hinton St George and went to school in Crewkerne! Small world.*
Lesley: *Ha-ha I lived in Reading too.*
Me: *I've also lived there and went to Earley St Peters School! This is too spooky!* **(I couldn't believe it!)**
Lesley: *I lived in Woodcote.* **(about 10 miles away)**
Me: *No way! Have you ever lived in Bournemouth? Or Plymouth?* **(I've moved around a bit)**
Lesley: *No not lived there but my son lives in New Milton.* **(about 20 miles away from Bournemouth)**
Me: *Close enough!*

I was so thrilled I put a Facebook post on her timeline which read; *Lesley Charlton to Lesley Charlton "Thanks Lesley Charlton"* (simple but I think it said it all) with a picture of me raising a glass to my new friend. To which she responded;

Lesley: *Lovely pic x*
Me: *Thank you. See what I mean about the hair? x*
Lesley: *YES, I DO! x*

I was delighted by our communications and the coincidences and although it was only a brief chat, I really felt like we'd connected. Imagine my surprise when, a week or so later, I received the following message;

Hi Lesley, I am getting married on 14th Feb this year but I will keep my name as Charlton on Facebook until after your birthday on 29th March. Hope you get all your wishes for the big 50. Maybe I should have done a bucket list when I was 50 lol xxx

To which I replied;

Hi Lesley. Wow congratulations and how romantic getting married on Valentine's Day. That is really lovely of you to stay as Charlton but if you want to change it that's absolutely fine as you're already an achievement on my Bucket List ... and it's never too late for you to start one! Have an amazing wedding. We are doing a tour of Ringwood Brewery on Valentine's Day but I will be thinking of you. xxx

We've kept in touch on and off since then. Once, I messaged her when we were driving to Devon, on the A303, as we were passing the turn off where she lived. I go that way from time to time and we've agreed that it would be nice to meet up one of these days. I'd like to think that will happen. I still can't believe how fortunate I was to find her when I did. If I'd left this one until later in the year, she'd have changed her surname and our paths would never have crossed. I guess it was just one of those things that was meant to be.

Chapter Three

(3rd February 2015)

Make a snow angel

This was a suggestion from one of my very kind friends! I put it on the List, not really thinking it would happen, as we don't generally get snow where we live and I had no plans to be visiting any snowy destinations. Kitzbühel would have been my only hope but I had nothing booked, as those visits are generally a bit last minute and I thought it would be a bit decadent to fly over just to make a snow angel! So, I was fully expecting to have to change this for something else later in the year.

Imagine my surprise when we woke up one morning to see a covering of snow on our deck. Mr C was just about to go out, to see a client. "I must get you to take a photo when you get back" I said. "I don't know how long I'm going to be, it may have melted by then" he replied. No time like the present then. Determined to go the whole hog, I grabbed my tankini (it's always by the back door, because of the hot tub), leapt outside, lay on the deck and made my snow angel. If I'd have given it a bit more thought I'd have leapt into the hot tub straight afterwards but Mr C was in such a hurry to leave, he only took a picture of me laying in the snow, so I had to take a picture of the actual angel myself, to prove I'd made one and by then I'd warmed up a bit, so didn't really feel the need for the "spa experience".

Like a lot of things, it's about seizing the moment. So, there you have it, the quickest box ticked and the shortest chapter to date ... although we're only on Chapter Three!!!

Chapter Four
(12th February 2015)
Finish your 40th Birthday photo album

There's something you should know about me, I'm REALLY good at starting things but REALLY bad at finishing them, which is why I'm keeping my fingers crossed that I actually finish this book. My fortieth (yes that's right, fortieth!) birthday photo album is a classic example. It all started with Linda's fortieth birthday. When Jim, her husband, asked her what she wanted for her big birthday her response was "A holiday with the girls" because she'd never had one! Probably not the answer that he was expecting but he went along with it and encouraged her to make it happen. I have always absolutely loved planning things like this for people and was honoured when she enlisted my help. I was recently widowed, so it was great having something exciting to look forward to. As it happened, we decided our destination was going to be Costa Teguise, Lanzarote, ironically not far from where I am as I write this. Steve's best friend, Bob, worked for a well-known hotel chain after leaving the Royal Navy and was often in a position to offer me certain perks of his job, such as ridiculously low rates on hotel rooms (which I was entitled to as a "family member", aka honorary sister) and even a safe, when they were upgrading one of their hotels.

The safe was a real asset. I'd experienced some security issues and the only semi-suitable thing I had, at the time, was a fireproof document box. Fine in the event of a fire but no use whatsoever in the event of a theft. So, the opportunity for a proper, secure safe was one I couldn't pass by. Having promised Steve he would look after me, Bob took on the role of man of the house when it came to all the jobs that I was too girlie to do on my own. His wife, Jude, had a Bobby Do hammer in their family home, which was a wooden cut out of a hammer, with a peg and magnet on the back and the words "Bobby Do" on the front. As Bob worked away a lot, any jobs that she needed him to do would be put on a list and clipped on the Bobby Do hammer on the fridge. On his return, he could catch up with the chores he had missed when he wasn't home. As Bob and Jude had taken me under their wings, Jude decided I should have a Bobby Do hammer too, so that when they/he popped down, whether I was there or not, he knew what needed doing. Installing the combination safe he'd acquired for me was put on the list and Bob duly came down and installed it for me. We'd discussed a secure location and it was put in situ, anchored to the floor and the wall so firmly that nobody was going to make off with that sucker!

I was thrilled with it but found it did eat through AA batteries at a rate of knots. Strangely, you had to open the safe to replace the batteries, which were located on the inside of the door, although this wasn't such a big problem, as it was in pretty regular use and would always give you a low battery warning in plenty of time. As it happened, for one reason or another, I stopped using it quite as regularly. Then, some years down the line, I went to get our passports out (luckily NOT just as we were leaving for the airport), only to find that, as I hadn't accessed it in such a long time, the batteries had gone completely flat and I had no idea how to get the door open. By now Mr C was on the scene and the obvious techie thing to do was Google it. He had the make and model but could find no instructions on the internet, so decided the best thing to do was ring the American manufacturers to ask for assistance. Working out the time difference, we got through to a very helpful lady in customer services, who assured us that it wasn't a problem and could be resolved very easily. Music to our ears. "What do we have to do?" we asked "Just call reception and they will send up the maintenance man with a bespoke power pack. He'll get it open for you straight away" was the reply. We thanked her profusely, hung up … and burst out laughing. We hadn't dared say the safe was no longer located in a hotel room, in case they traced it back and it was against the rules for us to have it in our house. Instead, we called the local locksmith, to find out how much it would be for them to open it. We were looking at over a hundred pounds! We then looked at the price of an angle grinder, which was considerably less, so it was off to a well-known DIY store for a bit of … DIY. Angle grinder purchased, it was put into action but even with all the windows and doors in the house open, the acrid smell of burning metal was choking. A few hours later, we still hadn't opened the safe but the angle grinder had given up the ghost.

I'm not overly proud of our next action but … we took it back to the store, explaining that we had only used it once (which was true) and it had stopped working (which was also true). Without a quibble, they offered a replacement, which we gratefully accepted and a few hours later, using angle grinder number two, the job was done. Through a large, jagged edged, hole the contents were safely (forgive the pun) removed and access was gained to the internal battery pack. Replacing the dead batteries meant the door could now be opened, giving full access to the internal fittings, enabling the now defunct safe to be removed from Bob's oh-so-secure fixings. It took weeks to completely get rid of the noxious smell, which seemed to cling to every item of soft furnishing, refusing to relinquish its grip. And of course, now I was back in my original predicament of not having a safe. Thoughtfully, for Christmas that year, Mr C bought me a new one, although the catch was that all my other presents were INSIDE and I had to work out the combination, from a series of clues, before I could retrieve them. We had a lot of fun that Christmas.

I appear to have digressed from my digression, so back to Linda's fortieth. I sort of took charge of arranging accommodation through Bob, who was still working for the hotel chain that, at the time, owned an unbranded hotel in Lanzarote. He could get us a really good deal so, as his "sister" I was able to secure us all a great bargain. Due to his generosity, Bob was subsequently christened Benefactor Bob, a title that has remained, even though he is now in retirement. Six of us signed up for the adventure in the Canary Islands. I produced a brochure, detailing where we were going, what we'd be doing, what to take, etc. I planned a daily programme of activities, together with games and quizzes, to keep us entertained along the way. We had an absolute blast. When we got back, everyone gave me copies of their photos which, together with tickets, leaflets and various mementoes, I used to produce a substantial album for Linda, as a reminder of the fun times we'd had.

The following year it was Maggie's fortieth. We were the same group of six and enlisting the help of Benefactor Bob again for our accommodation (of course), we booked her a surprise trip to Edinburgh. Similarly, on our return, I produced another scrap book type album for Maggie. The next year it was my turn. Benefactor Bob came up trumps yet again. This time, we were a slightly different group of girls and our numbers had swelled to eight and this time we were heading for Barcelona. The theme was "Pink" and the dress code was "Pink" so, obviously, we called ourselves the Pink Ladies and set off for a rather cool spring break in this wonderful city. We looked quite a sight, travelling around in our identical pink pashminas (to keep out the chill), resembling a group of pink Hare Krishnas. Once again, I produced brochures and planned lots of activities and once again, I got copies of everyone's photos and kept all the memorabilia. I bought two big pink photo albums ... and that's as far as I got. Ten years later, the photos were still in their packets, the mementos were still neatly filed and the albums were still in their plastic wrappers. As I said, great at starting things but not so good at finishing them.

Now, in my Bucket List year, the time had come to get the job done. I gathered the Pink Ladies together, sadly minus one, as Mr and Mrs Benefactor Bob have since retired to California and Jude couldn't be with us, to finally complete MY album. We drank pink Cava, ate pink Smarties, pink marshmallows and Pink Panther wafer biscuits and laughed all night. In some ways it was a good thing that I'd left it so long, as it was great fun reminiscing, although quite scary looking back at ourselves a decade ago. However, my mission was accomplished, the albums were complete and I could (finally) tick another one off the List.

Chapter Five

(15th - 18th March 2015)

Make a basket

This kind of all started when we were visiting my brother and his wife the previous November. Dee is VERY creative and enrols herself on a residential course at West Dean College once or twice a year. She was telling me about her latest booking and got the brochure out to show me. It looked amazing. Thumbing through the pages, I could see lots of things that interested me but one thing in particular had my name written all over it … Basket Making!

Now, I've always been a bit of a basket case (as friends and family will testify), in more ways than one. I have baskets for everything. I'm a bit like a wicker magpie, I just can't resist things made of pliable twigs. I'd always wanted to make my own baskets but appreciated that there's a bit more to it than twisting a few sticks together. However, THIS was the perfect opportunity to turn my dreams into reality. I ordered my own prospectus as soon as I got home. A couple of days later, I was in a coffee shop with my friend Jo, who is probably THE most creative person I know, full of enthusiasm at my findings and asking her if she wanted to join me. I nearly burst with excitement when she said yes! A couple of days after that, I popped in to see her for a cuppa, prospectus in hand. We checked our diaries and booked it there and then. This really was going to be one for the Bucket List.

On Mothering Sunday, we packed our bags (taking my Mother's Day gifts of Prosecco and chocolates from Josh with me ... in a basket of course), abandoned our children and set off for the picturesque college in West Sussex. We were like giggling schoolgirls as we checked into our room and opened the Prosecco. Once we'd unpacked, which took all of seconds, we went for a wander around to get our bearings and enjoy the tranquil, creative surroundings we found ourselves in. That evening, at the Welcome Meeting, we introduced ourselves to our tutor Mary Butcher, one of the nicest ladies you could ever meet, before having supper with her and our fellow students. By 8pm we were in the workshop and after a brief intro, we were straight into starting our first basket. My diary entry for that day was *"Jo and I were soooooo excited by the whole thing"* which sums it up perfectly.

As a bit of a back-story (here I go, off on my ramblings again), the previous summer, Mr C and I had been in France, touring around in Ruby (our beloved campervan if you remember). I was very envious of the elegant French ladies buying their fresh produce in the markets, when we shopped for provisions each day. Not because they were elegant, nor because they could shop for fresh produce daily but because they would put their purchases into their delightful, wheeled shopping baskets. You know the sort. Imagine a Granny Shopper (sorry Mum, I know you used one for years – in fact, we use one for the Isle of Wight Festival each year, they are so useful ...uh oh, what's happening to me?!?). Anyway, imagine a Granny Shopper that, instead of being made of tartan showerproof fabric ... was made of wicker! This is what the elegant French ladies were using. Each day I would drool over the different designs. Some had stick handles, some had hooped handles, some were lined with pretty fabric, some even had wicker lids with leather straps and buckle clasps. I was in awe. Mr C got used to me getting distracted each time we passed one. Imagine my absolute delight when, in a Tourist Information Centre one day (I'm a sucker for a Tourist Information Centre as our friends Craig and Caroline will confirm. Craig and I can never pass one without popping in, whilst Caroline and Kev like to "guess" what is available in the area … a constant source of hilarity), I found a leaflet about a place in Northern France, where you could go and watch baskets being made … and buy them … and the picture on the front of the leaflet was of a wheeled wicker shopping basket. It was clearly fate. I was destined to have one.

We were being a bit nomadic, with no real itinerary, so it would be easy to plan a route that would get us into the right area. I turned the leaflet over, to check the opening times. We'd only gone for a long weekend and were booked on the early morning ferry home on the Tuesday morning. The next time the workshop was open was going to be … Tuesday. I was mortified. However, we like a little jaunt to France now and then, so I was hopeful that another opportunity would present itself on future travels.

Fast forward a bit and here I am, booked on a basket making course, rather than a ferry to France. Communication with our tutor beforehand went like this;

7th January 2015 10.34pm
Hi Mary

My friend and I are booked onto your Baskets from Willow course at West Dean College in March. We are both beginners at basket making but are very enthusiastic and would love to make a French shopping trolley like the one below **(I attached a picture)**, *do you think that would be a possibility?*

Many thanks
Lesley

8th January 2015 8.44 am
Hi Lesley

Nice photo! Nice projects.
How much experience have you had? It is quite a big basket even for 3 days. The other problem is the set of wheels. I have one second-hand set one of you could buy (£10) which has handle and base with wheels all part of one unit, but you would need another unless you find walking sticks (often in charity shops) to incorporate into the baskets and then sets of pram wheels with axles to attach from below. That bit would have to be done at home afterwards.

We have the willow, we have thick stuff for the front leg. I am happy to guide you through it but would much prefer you to have had some willow experience first! Maybe you have. I hope that doesn't seem unreasonable. There are a number of ways in which we can make them to make it all a bit less difficult if necessary.

Please would you bring as many measurements as you can to give guidelines? Base shape and dimensions, height at stick and opposite, width at top, height at which weave changes (if you want the same sort of pattern) and anything else you can think of! I will bring my beaten-up one too.

Look forward to hearing your reactions and to meeting you in March.

Best wishes, Mary

<u>*8th January 2015 8.53am*</u> **(I was keen!!!)**
Hi Mary

Thank you for replying so promptly. Neither of us have ANY experience, which is why we wondered if this was ambitious but we would both love to make one at some stage. I have my Grandfather's walking stick that I would like to incorporate ... but no wheels, although I could probably source some. Would love your beaten-up one anyway, even if it is for a future project, if that is OK?

If you would prefer us to have some willow experience first that is absolutely fine, that's why I contacted you, to be guided by you.

As you can probably tell we are creatively ambitious and enthusiastic enough to try to run before we can walk!

Best wishes, Lesley

<u>8th January 2015 9.04am</u> **(she seemed keen too!)**
Lesley

I definitely approve of your last sentiment! But I think that a few round baskets, to get your hand in and sense the willow, might make for much more successful trolleys. Yes, I will bring my beaten-up one - a gentle reminder just before the course would be really helpful. I do file all the stuff I have to bring over but reminders are good! See what you think and we can go from there.

Best wishes, Mary

<u>12th March 2015 4.11pm</u> **(well she told me to remind her)**
Hi Mary

Here is the gentle reminder about the beaten-up French shopping trolley as per your email of 8th Jan.

Looking forward to starting our course on Sunday.

Best wishes, Lesley

<u>12th March 2015 6.33pm</u>
Thank you! I had remembered so far and will try to do so until it is in the car! Look forward to seeing you.

Mary

Fast forward again back to Jo and me, in the workshop, on the first night. Mary thought we had picked up the basics quite quickly, so was going to speak to the technician about making us some wooden bases, using her old beaten-up basket as a template. Result! We thought we were excited before but our excitement reached fever pitch at this news. That night in our room, tucked up in our single beds which faced each other across the room, we were so hyper it was ridiculous.

Day Two and the itinerary looked like this;

9.15am   Morning class starts

10.30am Coffee

11.00am Morning class continues

12.45pm Lunch

2.00pm   Afternoon class starts

3.30pm   Tea

4.00pm   Afternoon class continues

5.00pm   Class finishes

7.00pm   Dinner

8.15pm   Evening working with Mary until 9.15pm

10.00pm Workshop closes after unsupervised work

The workshop was open from 8am. We'd had breakfast and were waiting at the door. As the technician arrived with his keys to open up, we were like greyhounds out of a trap. We stayed until 10pm. Our first baskets, small shopping baskets with handles, were complete. They may have been a bit wonky to the trained eye but as a first attempt, we were euphoric and Mary was delighted with our efforts too. We were onto our second assignment, when she said the shopping trolleys were definitely a possibility! My diary entry for that night read *"So excited we couldn't sleep! Amazed with our achievements today. We were too energised to go to bed so, after dinner, we soothed our aching hands in the plastic, cream filled moisturising gloves Jo had brought for us, while drinking wine, eating chocolates and chatting about everything and everyone we had encountered today. A wonderful end to a wonderful day"*.

Day three and we were up really early, for a stroll around the grounds before breakfast and back in the workshop again as soon as it opened. By lunchtime, our second creations, this time we'd made shallow fruit baskets, were complete. Mary cast an approving eye and we got the news we were waiting for … she thought we were ready to start our shopping trolleys! Our faces ached from grinning so much, as we made a start on our mammoth projects.

Day four, we thought, was going to be a race against time, as this was our last day at West Dean and we were leaving at 4pm. However, we were determined and beavered away as if our lives depended on it. Against the odds, by the end of the course, we had completed three baskets … including our shopping trolleys. Mary was impressed by our dedication and determination. They may not be perfect, or stylish like the French ladies' versions but they were ours and we were so very proud. They were, however, enormous! Obviously, despite putting in four whole days, we are not the most experienced basket makers, so we ended up with something resembling the first pot you would throw on a potter's wheel. You know the sort, you throw a lump of clay at it, dig your thumbs in the middle and start to spin. The more you spin, the wider the pot becomes. Well, we'd started with bases the exact size of the one Mary had brought with her as a template but the more we weaved, the wider the top became. You could probably fit a weekly family shop in these monsters but what an achievement. We headed home, like children coming home from their early days at school, clutching sugar paper paintings and junk models for parents to marvel over while the little ones grin from ear to ear. Only we were clutching baskets ... still grinning from ear to ear.

I put mine (the baskets not sugar paper paintings and junk models) out on display for a good few days, leaving them hanging around, in the hope that people would notice them and comment (that's the five-year-old in me). How chuffed was I when, three days later, Matt, our plumber was fixing a new kitchen tap and Kath popped in for a cup of tea. Kath made all the right noises, like a good friend should, picking each one up in turn and finding nice things to say about all of them (well, she is a primary school teacher). Matt's ears pricked up. "Wow, you made those?" he said. "Yes, I did" says me, smugly. "That's fantastic, you see I've built these wardrobes at home and I want four identical made-to-measure baskets to fit into them. If I give you the dimensions, would you make them for me? I'll pay you!". I had to let him down gently and it took quite a while for him to accept that his request was way (way, WAY) beyond my capabilities. I did email Mary to ask if she could recommend anyone and she gave me some details to pass on to him. I also sent her a picture of me in Marrakech, surrounded by baskets (I told you I couldn't help myself) but you've got a couple of chapters to go before you read about that little adventure! Of course, in true Lesley fashion, my shopping trolley isn't quite finished! It does have a handle. I used my Grandad's walking stick, which is of huge sentimental value, so seemed quite fitting. However, Jo and I have not yet sourced the wheels to attach to the bases. It is on our "to do" list though, so one day they will be finished and we did make the baskets, so I can tick this one off my list with supreme confidence.

Chapter Six

(22nd - 24th March 2015)

Sleep in a lighthouse

Who hasn't wanted to sleep in a Lighthouse? I know I always have. This was supposed to be the entry which Mr C had put on the List, as "Mr C's Surprise" (he knows me so well) ... but I'd already bagged that one. I Googled "unusual places to stay" and came up trumps with the Belle Tout Lighthouse at Beachy Head, offering themed rooms, including the Keepers Loft. Their website description was;

"The original Lighthouse Keeper's bunk room is round with feature brick walls and fireplace. Intimate and quirky, climb up the original ladder to the double loft bed. Small window with a view of Beachy Head Lighthouse and coastline. En-suite facilities including shower".

Oh yes, this ticked all my boxes. I like intimate and quirky, I've never stayed in a round room before and I LOVED the idea of climbing up a ladder to our double bed with views out to sea. Sold to the lady with the Bucket List!

The lighthouse had been through a few transitions in its life. It had been bought by the BBC, who used it for "Life and Loves of a She-Devil", used as a family home and even moved 17 metres back from the edge of the cliff, when it was threatened by coastal erosion. We had to stay a minimum of two nights (well sometimes you just have to make sacrifices) and received a warm welcome on arrival. I think the correct phrase would be that it has been "sympathetically restored". An example of this is the original lamp room. The lamp has been removed and the room is now home to a cosy seating area, with three-hundred-and-sixty-degree views. You can while away hours up there, just watching the world go by. Telescopes and binoculars are supplied, to extend the panorama and it is a truly incredible spot for viewing spectacular sunsets.

Our room was really original, even the en-suite was curved. Climbing into the bunk was, shall we say, "interesting", as the ascent was up a completely vertical ladder. The bed itself wouldn't suit anyone who was claustrophobic, as you could reach out and touch the ceiling with your hands when you laid down. However, it was comfy, cosy and most definitely quirky. On the first night, we went to a nearby village for supper. As one of us had to drive, we decided to wait until we returned to the lighthouse to have a drink. Taking a couple of bottles of wine up to the lantern room, we lit candles in storm lanterns filled with shells (in addition to baskets, candles and shells are my other favourite things). I was in seventh heaven.

The lighthouse can accommodate up to twelve guests but as there was nobody else in the lantern room that night, Mr C brought the little portable speaker up with us, so we could play our music. "What do you want to listen to?" he asked. By now, the wine was flowing nicely, so "Something we can sing along to" was my response. We listened to some good old eighties tunes and sang along at the top of our voices, after all, we were at the pinnacle of a lighthouse, on the edge of a cliff and nobody can hear you up there! I'm not sure how many hours we were there but when we came back down to the very cosy lounge, which was on the same floor as our bedroom, we noticed a lovely log burner (hmmm ... log burner ... that would be nice but where would we put one in our house? Hold that thought), which was still glowing with warm embers, obviously having been enjoyed by other guests. We stoked it up a bit and basked in the ambience, before retiring to bed.

The next morning, at breakfast, we got chatting to a couple who we'd met briefly in the lantern room the previous afternoon. We exchanged pleasantries about where we'd eaten the night before and what we thought of the Belle Tout. We told them about our candlelit evening in the lantern room and the good old sing-along we'd had. "We know" they said. "How could you know?" we asked, "We were two floors up a stone staircase with a substantial door at the bottom which was closed". They laughed, "It also has a large metal flue from the log burner in the lounge which goes up through the lantern room, so while we were sitting in front of the fire, we could hear your singing echoing through the fireplace!". Unperturbed, we replied "You should have come and joined us", to which their response was "You seemed to be having far too much fun for us to spoil it". Well, at least we'd found out who'd lit the fire for us.

The next day, I found a leaflet, about being a shepherd for the night at the local Seven Sisters Sheep Centre. "I'd love to spend a night helping with lambing" I told Mr C but he sensibly replied that it was a bit late in the afternoon to enquire, as the number of places were limited and it would probably have been booked up ages ago. It would have been a good one for the Bucket List though and it would have taken me back to my senior school days in Somerset, where, living in a farming community, Rural Science was a compulsory subject in the first year, learning things such as how to castrate piglets and how to cut their eye teeth, to protect the sows when they were suckling.

I wasn't born in the country but I soon adapted to living in a rural community. After school, I would help the village herdsman with the cattle, even learning how to show pedigree bulls (Barney was my favourite, I still have his rosettes in the loft somewhere) at the Melplash Show. While my friends were competing in gymkhanas (although I did love horse riding too), I was shampooing and backcombing over a tonne of prime beef, preparing him for the show ring … but that really is a story for another book.

We did call in to the Seven Sisters Sheep Centre, on our way home the following day. I told the lady I was sad to have missed the opportunity to be a shepherd for the night. "Oh, you should have come along" she said, "We didn't have anyone booked in for last night". Mr C slunk away into a corner. However, we enjoyed our daytime visit and we did get to bottle-feed the orphaned lambs, so all was not lost.

Chapters Seven & Eight
(3rd - 8th April 2015 … supposedly but read on)

Visit Marrakech and go White Water Rafting in the High Atlas Mountains

&

(5th April 2015)

Sleep under the stars

Many years ago, a very dear friend, Pete, late husband of my fellow basketeer Jo, told me the story of a Moroccan adventure he had been on with "the boys", staying in Marrakech, then heading up into the High Atlas Mountains, where they went white water rafting. I was enthralled. I have always loved and been fascinated by Africa (something I am trying to educate Mr C in the ways of … and winning I think) and this sounded like an amazing trip. At the time, Josh was still young but a couple of years later, I remember asking Pete if he thought Josh was old enough to give it a go. He said he thought he would be able to cope, so I started looking into it. In fact, I began communicating with the guy who'd arranged Pete's trip. However, as is often the way in our busy lives, things sometimes get in the way and because there is only a small(ish) window each year when the water is high enough for rafting, for one reason or another other events always seemed to take priority and so it just never happened.

Remember us ladies making trips to celebrate our fortieths? Well, now we were all grown up and celebrating our fiftieths … and the boys had got involved too! For Jim's fiftieth, we planned a "Surprise trip to Berlin", except it didn't actually turn out to be a surprise. I'd been grilling Mr C about the importance of not saying anything about it to Jim and how we had to keep it an absolute secret. Then, late one evening, in the village pub, sitting around an open fire after sampling a few real ales (I blame the ale and the fire), with Jim sitting right next to me … I let the cat out of the bag. Me of all people! The queen of discretion. The one who had been SO insistent that we keep it as a big surprise. I was mortified to say the least and rushed off to the loo in tears. Luckily, Linda forgave me (I think) and Jim said, very charitably "At least I have something to look forward to", bless him.

Despite the lack of a surprise element, we had an absolutely fantastic time, for me especially as I hadn't been back since the wall came down. For John's fiftieth, he'd hired some rigid ribs for the day, each with a skilled crew, who took us on an exhilarating ride around the Solent, as far west as the Needles and as far east as the Forts. It was fast and full on. We had breakfast in Cowes and lunch in the Medina. The guys piloting the boats had us doing doughnuts and criss-crossing in front of each other at speed. The word exciting really does not do it justice. For Linda's fiftieth, we went up to Scotland. Four couples flew from Southampton, our local airport. Unbeknown to Linda, until we presented her with her and Jim's on the day, each couple had matching "Harold and Hilda" woollen jumpers. Each jumper had a rather unflattering photo transfer of Linda stitched on the front, topped off with little matching bobble hats, that Maggie had hand knitted. We were met at Glasgow airport by another two couples, each sporting their similarly customised pullovers. It's amazing how quickly you forget what you and your fellow companions are wearing and it just becomes the norm. We kept wondering why people were looking at us … until we looked at each other! In addition, Linda had bought a set of celebrity face masks. You know the sort, cardboard ones with cut out eyeholes. It's actually quite spooky how convincing a two-dimensional mask can be and you wouldn't believe the things Bruce Forsyth got up to with Holly Willoughby in our B&B one night … all in the name of a good photo of course.

We had a great few days, touring around Scotland in a minibus, often with Her Majesty The Queen and Prince Philip sitting up front, also sporting "those jumpers". I think one of the funniest games we played in the pub that weekend was "Which body part is it?". If you haven't tried it, you should. Each couple take turns to disappear to the toilets together (if you're in a public house but if you're not, any other room will suffice), then secretly take a close-up photo of a particular body part. They then return to the table, pass the camera around and the others have to guess which "part" it is. It's not quite as weird as it sounds, you'd be amazed how indistinguishable the tip of your finger, or crook of your arm can look when you take a close-up. Obviously though, the object of the game is to make it look as rude as possible. It took a bit of explaining to the bar staff (why we were making endless trips to the loo followed by a series of groans, gasps and hysterical laughter on our return) but I'm pretty sure we're now legendary in a certain part of Scotland.

For Maggie's fiftieth, she took us to the Gower Peninsular. Six of us in a cottage for a long weekend. Well, it was six-and-a-half of us really. You see, Maggie had given me a little beanbag frog, that she used to make for her children when they were young. She thought I might like to use it as a template to make my own, as I was expanding my Love and Sparkles range (I'm still wondering why it failed as a business venture aren't you?). Anyway, I thought it would be fun to make a "Little Maggie" from one of these cute beanbags, complete with a picture of her face (another photo transfer, as per Linda's jumpers) and knitted curly hair. It actually turned out to be the most horrific thing you have ever seen in your life but it gave us some great photo opportunities and she, Little Maggie, came with us wherever we went … much to Big Maggie's horror.

The ongoing game that weekend was the "soldiers game". At the beginning of the trip, I produced a small bag containing six toy soldiers, each exhibiting a different pose. Everyone had to close their eyes and randomly pick one. Well, I say randomly but actually we made sure Maggie's soldier was the one in the prone position. Wherever we were, whenever somebody shouted "Take cover" you had to assume the position of your toy soldier. Poor Maggie, we had her laying down in some awful places. Mind you, she got her revenge … by booking us into an Activity Centre for the day.

The main objective at the Activity Centre was to complete, what they claim to be, the Muddiest Assault Course in the World (which was actually a lot of fun). However, the other activities throughout the day included things like Team Building ... for just the six of us (who have actually known each other for many years – very useful), where they had us making up team songs, doing relay races and executing pencil rolls down a hill (because of course, we were obviously five and not fifty). We also had problem solving competitions (the girls won) and INDOOR archery, which, we had to admit, was a first. The room wasn't a lot bigger than our lounge (which isn't very big) and the arrows were as straight as a shepherd's crook. You took your life in your hands firing one of those things. All in all it was probably a good format ... if only they'd thought about how to tailor it, depending on the group.

Then, as a "special treat", Maggie paid extra for us to go horse riding. Except it wasn't really horse riding, it was more horse walking. In pairs, according to size, one of us would sit on a horse and the other would hold the horse's bridle. In addition, one of the stable girls would hold the bridle on the other side, quite frankly rendering the non-seated person useless, as we walked along a muddy path on top of a hill. Once we reached a gap in the hedge, leading to open fields (ideal for a bit of gentle cantering), we thought things would liven up a bit ... but we just turned around and walked back to the stables, where the "rider" and "walker" changed places, before the whole process was repeated. It was almost as exciting as riding a donkey on Blackpool Beach. Almost ... but not quite. As we led our mounts back to the stables, following the second circuit, we were greeted by a group of excitable under-tens, getting ready for one little girl's pony trekking birthday party, who looked pretty surprised to see a bunch of old farts, doing the same thing. I'm sure you get the picture. Poor Maggie was mortified but we've dined out on that story ever since.

Actually, although that was a funny story, I think the funniest tale from that weekend was when Maggie, being very organised, pre-booked a taxi to take us to a local restaurant for dinner. Both the taxi and the dinner were great. However, on the Saturday night before our trip to Wales, Maggie was reclining on her sofa at home in Hampshire, when her phone rang. The gentleman said her taxi was outside. Unfortunately, he was outside the house we'd rented in Wales for the weekend … the following weekend! Ironically, when the taxi actually did collect us a week later, it was the same driver who Maggie had spoken to on the phone. We haven't let her live that one down either!

Back to me and the bar was set, sort of, so when it came to MY fiftieth, I knew I had to pull something out of the bag. It was time to resurrect my investigations about the trip to Morocco. I sensed that not everyone was as enthusiastic as me but after painting a very colourful picture of how wonderful it would be, the six musketeers, perhaps with some trepidation, were signed up for it. They could have said no, so I have no sympathy I'm afraid. I think, on reflection, everyone had a good time … after the mental scars had healed. I've almost (but not quite) forgotten some of the comments when we got back, like Jim saying he's never going to Morocco again as long as he lives and John saying it will take him a long time to trust a Moroccan gentleman again, or words to that effect but I'm not going to elaborate on these quotes, instead I'm going to start at the beginning.

Of course, we had the obligatory "Tour T-Shirts", created by my so-called friends, with a lovely picture (photo transfer – we should have bought shares in that stuff) of me on the front, aged about nine (thanks Mum) and a list of all our gigs to date, just like a rock group tour t-shirt, on the back, which was a definite talking point. Mine was pink (of course) and everyone else's were blue. So, let's just say Morocco knew we'd arrived, although not many people associated me with the image of the little girl in bunches, emblazoned on our chests, asking who it was and not being totally convinced when everyone pointed to me. We probably looked more like a "find this missing child" campaign.

Unconcerned, we checked into a lovely little riad, in the heart of the Medina in Marrakech. The manager was a bit of a Mr Ben character as, throughout our stay, he seemed to pop up and be working wherever we were … and I mean WHEREVER. He was really helpful though, leading us through the souks and the alleyways of the Medina, getting us to take photos as we went, so that we would always be able to find our way home. A bit like a modern-day Hansel and Gretel, leaving a trail of breadcrumbs but using pictures instead … and having more success.

We settled in and on the first evening, had a fabulous meal, in a little oasis within the Medina (booked and escorted to by Mr Ben - of course). The next day, we packed our essentials into dry bags, leaving the rest of our belongings at the riad and set off to meet the rafting team. Unfortunately, the transport which was due to take us to the Atlas Mountains, owned by Water by Nature, the adventure travel company we'd booked with, had a catastrophic failure. We waited on the edge of the Medina while alternative arrangements were made, which turned out to be hiring a totally unsuitable vehicle and keeping the newly recruited driver in the dark about the terrain that lay ahead. I suppose, with hindsight, the signs of how our adventure would progress were already there but blissfully unaware, we soldiered forth.

The journey into the mountains was only supposed to take a couple of hours or so but it became very clear, very quickly, that it was going to take longer and I mean a LOT longer. To some extent, we were placated by the scenery, which was spectacular. We'd never expected it to be so green, or for there to be such a carpet of vibrantly coloured spring flowers. At lunchtime, we stopped by a stunning waterfall where, we all agreed, we had the best tagine ever. However, as the roads deteriorated so did everybody's mood, particularly that of our press-ganged driver. He was not impressed when the route took us over a rickety bridge and onto an unmade track. In fact, when the unmade track turned into a steep gravel path, he refused to go any further. He was getting very agitated, babbling away at a hundred miles an hour and gesticulating, so we disembarked, unloaded all the kit onto the side of the road ... and he was off, without a backward glance. Luckily, we were closer to our destination than we'd thought and a short time later, a Land Rover came, from camp, to collect the equipment and luggage. Unfortunately, there wasn't room for us ... so we had to walk the rest of the way. "All part of the adventure" I kept telling our team.

However, when we finally got there, all was soon forgotten, as the camp was quite something. Situated right on the bank of the Ahansal River, it was very efficiently organised, with a rustic seating area around the campfire, a kitchen-come-bar, a simple filtration system with a foot pump to provide running water for washing your hands, a large Bedouin tent that could accommodate multiple occupants and a couple of small modern tents. The dunny was impressive too. Situated away from the camp, a stone lined path led the way up a little hill to, what could best be described as, a wicker tent (you see - baskets again), with a large cloth flap that you could pull down over the doorway for modesty, not that there was anyone around to see you. Inside, was a toilet seat on a bench, over a long drop ... a VERY long drop!

We helped unload the gear from the Land Rover and set about deciding what our sleeping arrangements would be. The small modern tents were quickly snapped up by other participants (lightweights) on the tour, so the alternatives were communal sleeping in the Bedouin tent ... or sleeping under the stars. Well, it just had to be done, as this too was on my Bucket List. So, we set up our beds (a sleeping bag on a camping mat), all six of us on the bank, as close to the fast-flowing river as was safe

... and there we were, checked into our million-star hotel for the night. I couldn't wait for it to get dark. The thought of lying there, high up on the mountain, with no light pollution, gazing up at the galaxy, was so exciting. Unfortunately, it didn't quite happen like that.

After a fabulous supper (and some over-priced beers) around the campfire, it was time for bed. Snuggled up in our individual cocoons on the riverbank, with the sound of the water rushing by, we were anticipating the wonders of the night sky above us ... except, that night had the biggest, brightest full moon I have ever seen. It was like sleeping under a floodlight. The good thing was, when you wanted to go to the dunny, you certainly didn't need a torch! Oh well, no astrological extravaganza tonight but there was always tomorrow.

The next morning, we were up early, had breakfast and were ready for the off. Only, yet again, things did not go according to plan. There had been an incredible amount of snowfall in the mountains that winter, followed by incredibly high temperatures in the spring, which meant the melt had been the most dramatic for many years. In fact, the river was at its highest level for over three decades. What would normally happen on this trip was that you would set off from the camp we were at and spend the day paddling downstream. Half-way down the river, you would make camp for the night, then the following day, paddle down the remainder of the river, into the lake at the bottom. Following lunch on the water, there would be an opportunity to play around on the lake for a while, before meeting up with the transport, for the return journey to the city. With conditions as they were, there was no way we would be able to do this, as the water was just too high and running far too fast. The level was allegedly dropping though, so there was still a hope that we would be able to paddle downstream the following day.

This meant that because of Mother Nature's unpredictability, our options for that day were a) transport us down to the lake and just play around on kayaks or b) transport us and the rafts upstream and raft back to the camp we were currently at. As we were there for the rafting, the unanimous decision was to head upstream. The Land Rovers were loaded and we set off along a very bumpy, very steep track, with a sheer drop on one side. It was definitely not for the faint-hearted as the hairpin bends were … interesting! However because there was not enough room for everyone inside the vehicles, our raft guides had to sit inside the rafts, which were perched on top of our transport, lashed down with ropes – now THAT is hard core. Once we were all safely at our launch point, we were kitted out in wetsuits, buoyancy aids and safety gear, then allocated to rafts (the six of us were all together) and given a briefing.

We carried our rafts to the riverbank, edged out into the water, jumped in and then, as quick as a flash, we were off. The water looked like creamy hot chocolate, a clear sign of how rough it was upstream and was running so fast you didn't get time to take in the scenery. At that speed, when you looked downstream, you could actually see just how steep the angle of the river was. It was very obvious that we were rushing downhill, which was a little surreal. Normally, when you go rafting, you drift for a bit, paddle gently for a bit, then paddle like mad when you hit the rapids. On this run, you hardly needed to paddle at all, apart from to steer, as the rafts went thundering down of their own accord. When we got to each rapid, the raft-master gave very precise instructions about when to paddle, as he navigated our way through and then powered us out. We had a couple of close scrapes. At one point, we popped out of a rapid with such force that, despite our best efforts, we were on a collision course with a rocky overhang on the riverbank and had to lay almost flat, using our paddles to fend off the impending boulders, with inches to spare. It was an exhilarating ride and we covered twenty-five kilometres in about forty-five minutes, finishing with a handbrake turn, to get the rafts into calmer waters as we approached camp.

Well, that was the morning done then. What next? It was suggested that, after lunch, we go back and do a second run. The water was apparently still dropping but not enough for us to head downstream and because of the speed of the flow and the impact it was having on the local topography, nobody was quite sure if it was passable anyway, as there may be debris inhibiting us. Everyone was up for the re-run, which was just as fast, only this time we were able to take in a bit more of our surroundings, like the monkeys playing in the trees ... and the locals looking at us as if we were mad, as we passed their village. Apparently, most locals don't swim and think it's crazy to be on the river.

Back at camp, a decision was made to send the guy in the safety kayak down to the lake to check the route and see if it would be possible for us to do that part of the run the following day. Meanwhile, all the rest of us could do was chill out and wait. So, we ate, drank and were very, very merry. That evening there was a little cloud cover and the temperature had dropped quite a bit, so we made the decision to sleep in the Bedouin tent, after all, we could always pop outside to look at the stars. Except we couldn't because by nightfall, there was total cloud cover, which meant we couldn't even see the moon! It was black and I mean pitch black. So much so, that when you set off for the dunny, not only did you have to wear your head torch but you needed a hand-held torch too and that was just to find the line of stones that marked the pathway. Talk about going from one extreme to the other.

By morning, the decision had been made that completing the run was unachievable. It had taken the safety kayaker just three hours to reach the lake and there were lots of fallen trees along the way, making it impossible for the rafts to pass. It hadn't been the rafting trip we thought it was going to be but we'd certainly had an exciting time. We boarded the repaired bus for the long journey back to Marrakech, to spend a couple of days in the city, before heading home ... or so we thought.

Back in the Medina, it was time to address another one of the challenges, set by my friends, that I had to complete in Morocco. I had to arrange a Hamam, a traditional process of cleansing and relaxation, for us. Of course, I enlisted the help of our faithful Mr Ben. He said he knew just the place and gave us a leaflet, listing the menu of treatments. We all decided to go for the full works and as it was a special occasion, we thought we'd go the whole hog and reserve the private jacuzzi on the roof, as an added treat at the end. Mr Ben booked it for us and escorted us there. Even though it was literally just around the corner, with the multitude of winding alleyways, we wouldn't have found our way without him. From the outside it was a deceptive, unremarkable building, with a large plain wooden door but inside, it was a luxurious and tranquil retreat.

We were served mint tea and asked to decide the order we would like to go in, as they were going to take us one couple at a time. The first couple were shown to the changing room, emerging a short time later in robes and slippers, before being whisked away by the attentive ladies. Mr C and I said we would go last and because of this, for some reason, we were offered "the bath". We didn't really understand what it was, or why we'd been offered it but we said yes anyway. Well, why not? When our turn came, we went into the changing room, where we were presented with our robes, slippers and paper knickers. Now, when I say paper knickers, what I mean is paper shorts for the gentleman and a paper thong for the lady. Apparently one size fits all. Does it? Does it really? Linda, Maggie and I are all quite different sizes and I'm not sure they fitted us all in quite the same way.

Once "dressed", we were taken into the next room, where they sat us on, what could best be described as, thrones. Grand chairs regally situated on a plinth draped in organza. We were given a series of aromatics to smell. From our preferences, they put a blend of intoxicating scents together for us. Then it was on to the next room, where we received a wonderful foot massage, whilst being liberally sprayed with a mist of orange blossom water. It was very enjoyable but we could hear a lot of giggling coming from further down the corridor. Linda and Jim emerged from one of the rooms with big grins and Linda said "You're going to love that" but before we could ask what "that" was, we were ushered into another room, containing two baths. The lady removed our robes and helped each of us into a bath. Do paper knickers survive being soaked in a bath? We were about to find out. She turned the music up, the lights down and left us to it. We're not sure how long we were in there and to begin with, we were just lying there, waiting for something to happen … but nothing did. It was exactly what they'd offered us … a bath. I guess they thought we were the grubbiest ones of the group and yes, amazingly paper knickers do survive a bath!

After an unknown but seemingly prescribed, amount of time, the lady came back into the room and helped us out of the bath in turn (strange but not unpleasant), dressing us back in our robes. She took us to the next room, removing our robes once again as we entered, which was a little alarming as the door was wide open and we could hear the others approaching down the corridor. Luckily, the door was closed in time to save our modesty. This room was a bit like a steam room, with an L shaped, low-level, stone bench along one side and a trough in the corner, which had hot water constantly running into it. She gestured for Mr C to sit on the shorter part of the bench and for me to lay, face down, on the longer part. She then proceeded to lather me up with a wonderfully rich, oily, black soap. Next, she used an exfoliating glove, to give me a really good scrub. As I looked over my shoulder, bearing in mind I was face down, I could see lots of dark flecks or fibres. I assumed this was from the soap, or bits of the exfoliating glove but later found out it was several layers of my skin!!! She rinsed me off with buckets of hot water from the trough, which was actually really nice and I certainly felt clean and relaxed ... until she gestured for me to turn over. I'm not sure who's eyes were wider, mine or Mr C's. I can honestly say I have never had my boobs, or indeed any part of my frontage, so well cleaned by another woman in my whole life. She was thorough, I'll give her that.

Mr C didn't know where to look ... or should I say, where it was appropriate to look. I kept thinking, any minute now she's going to say something like "You pay extra for your husband to watch?" but thankfully, she didn't. It was hard not to laugh, purely because I hadn't really thought about what to expect and even if I had, I don't think it would have been that. Again, she doused me with the buckets of hot water, then helped me sit up. Next, she washed my hair and drowned, I mean rinsed, ... no, I do actually mean drowned, me with more buckets of water then signalled for us to swap places. Now it was my turn to watch!

Mr C lay face down and looked very relaxed, as she soaped his back and shoulders. He didn't look quite so relaxed when she rammed her exfoliating-gloved hand down the back of his shorts. In fact, he looked more like a rabbit caught in headlights. I knew exactly what he was thinking ... "is she going to do the same when I'm laid on my back?" Luckily, she didn't!

After our deep cleanse, we were taken to a lovely warm room, to dry off before putting our robes back on. Then, we were taken to a dimly lit room, containing two beds, for our massage. It was extremely relaxing. So relaxing in fact, that when they'd finished, leaving us swaddled in towels and with the lights turned down even further, Mr C was snoring peacefully. Feeling very mellow from the whole experience, we eventually joined the others on the rooftop terrace. I think the general consensus was "unexpected but most enjoyable".

They brought us more mint tea, then apologised profusely because the jacuzzi was out of action, meaning we wouldn't be able to use it after all. Oh yes, the jacuzzi, we'd forgotten all about that. There it was, in the corner. I guess, when they said it would have been for our "private use", they meant they'd have pulled the screens around, to stop anyone else on the terrace from seeing us. Then it dawned on us, under our robes, we were still only wearing our paper knickers. If it had been working, we would have all been in there together … in just our "one size doesn't fit all" underwear. I know we're good friends but even friendships have limits. Thank goodness it was out of action and we didn't have to test those limits! Having a good laugh at our narrow escape, we all agreed it was the perfect way to finish our holiday … or was it?

At the end of this pretty chilled last day, Mr Ben called for a six-seater taxi, to take us to the airport. We said our goodbyes and he mentioned something about having to hang around because his incoming guests had been delayed but we thought nothing of it. Wistfully looking out at the vibrant, exotic city, as we left the Medina our thoughts were already turning to what needed to be done when we got home. Arriving at the modern airport, things seemed pretty calm ... until we discovered our flight had been cancelled. The organisation wasn't great and people were already getting agitated. It transpired that we all had to join a queue, to speak to one poor lady, sitting alone behind a desk, who would tell us what our options were. They'll sort it soon enough we thought, determined not to be those people that get really stressed about it and make a mountain out of a molehill.

When, after forty minutes or so, she had only seen a couple of passengers, we realised we were a long way down the queue and this was going to take forever. Of course, news filtered back down the line about what our options actually were. Apparently, the French air traffic controllers were on strike again, bless them, so we could either get our money back and make our own way home (taxis, trains, ferries, etc - a logistical nightmare), stay in the airport (although it was a forty-eight hour strike, which had only just started), or let the airline put us up in a hotel until a suitable flight was available. One chap managed to get the last seat on a plane headed for Rome and thought he would take his chances and try to make his way home from there but what were the chances of us getting six seats on a plane, to anywhere? The problem is, to return to our little island from North Africa, you pretty much have to travel through French airspace, whichever route you choose. We decided to take the hotel option ... until we heard that they would not be allocating hotel accommodation until they had seen everybody in the queue!

By now it was well into the evening and it was still a very long queue. Also, the idea of being stuck in a big modern hotel, on the outskirts of Marrakech, for a good few days, did not appeal, so we made a group decision and called Mr Ben. If we couldn't get out of the country, surely his new guests couldn't get in! We dialled his number and explained the situation. "Get in a taxi and come home" he said, "We can sort this out". His confidence was reassuring and at least we knew we'd be back at "our" riad and even though we knew it would be at our own expense, our rooms were so cheap it was worth it. With an ever-so slightly smug look on our faces, we said farewell to our fellow travellers and went outside to find a taxi.

It's all quite civilised at Marrakech Airport, there's a rank and prices are displayed on a board, with fixed costs for both large and small taxis. Obviously, we wanted a large taxi. We approached the man who appeared to be in charge and requested one large taxi, for the six of us. As the next taxi on the rank, which happened to be the same size as all the other taxis, moved forward he escorted us towards it. We explained again that we needed a big taxi. "Yes, yes. This big taxi" was the response. We pointed out that there were six of us. "No problem", came the reply and with that, several gentlemen started loading our luggage into the boot of the not-overly-large saloon car. There was a lot of loud, fast Arabic being spoken and everyone was talking at once but they all seemed to know what they were doing. With the luggage piled high and the boot lid open, ropes appeared from somewhere and our bags were, apparently, secured. "What about us?" We stood shrugging our shoulders, much to the amusement of the men. "Yes, yes. Come" they said, ushering us into the vehicle. John, Jim, Mr C and I were squeezed into the back seat, with Linda and Maggie squished together in the single, front passenger seat ... and with that, we were off. Clearly the prices of the large and small taxis depended on the number of people rather than the physical size of the car! Seat belts were obviously not compulsory and would probably have been unnecessary anyway because in the event of a collision, I don't think we'd have budged, we were packed in so tightly. All we could do was laugh, as we sped our way through rush-hour, which is pretty much every hour in Marrakech, back to the drop off point, where Mr Ben was waiting to greet us with open arms.

Resigned to the fact that there was nothing to be achieved at that time of night, all we could do was have a meal and sleep on it. The following morning John went into action. He was on a mission. While he phoned various airlines, his daughter Jennie, back in the UK, was on both the phone and the internet simultaneously. Between them, they were trying to secure six tickets back to the UK, as soon as possible, without having to pay ridiculous prices. Mr C and I just sat back and watched without getting involved ... and there was a jolly good reason for that. We had only planned to be away for five nights and half of that was due to be in the High Atlas Mountains, where you wouldn't get a phone signal (wrong) and you wouldn't want to take any electronic stuff on a raft as you moved from camp to camp (wrong) and you wouldn't want to leave valuables in your luggage which would be left in a random locker/office somewhere while you were away rafting (wrong again). So it had made perfect sense, at the time, to leave every piece of technology at home. Who needs technology twenty-four-seven these days anyway? We'd also thought that it would be quite therapeutic to be gadgetless for a few days ... unless, of course, you were to get stranded in North Africa! That's why we had to leave it to someone else to get us home. Mr C and I were completely tech free.

Flights finally booked for five days later (and that was the earliest flights we could secure), the stress was off, as there was actually nothing more we could accomplish, apart from make the most of our extended holiday. One of our favourite things to do, was to go up on the roof of our riad with a nice cold beer, where we would relax on the floor cushions for a reading. We'd had a couple of afternoons up there, with me reading aloud from my *Berlitz Pocket Guide to Marrakech*, while the others, lulled by my dulcet tones (obviously), dozed in the sunshine. However I'd already read that publication, every single word of it, from cover to cover and there are only so many times you need to know all those things, especially as we had now actually experienced most of them. Of course, we hadn't packed our Kindles (part of our "no technology" plan), or a book (when would we have time to read on such an action-packed holiday with friends?!?) other than a travel guide. Actually, Linda had decided she would take her Kindle but they are not the easiest of things to share and if I'm honest, I think everyone had had enough of me reading aloud by then, so that wasn't going to be an option.

The only other person with a book, a good old-fashioned paperback, was Maggie. So, as abhorrent as this will be to all you book lovers out there, when faced with this true state of emergency, there was only one thing to do. The book had to be sacrificed! Maggie was already a few chapters in, so she tore out the part she had finished and passed it on, so that we could read it in tag fashion, a few chapters at a time. The poor book was slaughtered but it didn't die in vain. There was much hilarity as we all tried to read at the same speed because you didn't want to be the one holding up the passing on of the next section. Likewise, you did not want to finish your bit and have nothing to read until the person behind you had finished. Synchronised reading is a fine art, which our little group has managed to perfect. Of course, we didn't spend the whole time reading "the book", we had five days to fill, so we had to pace ourselves.

Poor Linda wasn't at all well, in fact, right up until the night before we'd left home, we weren't even sure if she'd be coming with us. She was so poorly but she soldiered on and assured me afterwards that she was glad she'd persevered. With the excitement of Marrakech, the rafting and the cancelled flight, it all caught up with her and she decided she needed some rest. Being the supportive friends we were ... we left her to her own devices, booking a taxi (small, large - they're all the same) to take us to the coast for the day. Jim politely declined the invitation to join us and did the dutiful husband thing, staying behind to administer medications and TLC ... while the rest of us buggered off.

It was a great day out (sorry you missed it Linda and Jim ... but we did show you the photos), one of the highlights of which was stopping by the side of the road, on the way to Essaouria, to marvel at trees full of goats! It was one of the most bizarre things I've ever seen.

There must have been over twenty goats in each tree, apparently just standing there, balanced on impossibly precarious branches and they weren't big trees either. I've since learned that, grown almost exclusively in Morocco, the Argania is now a rare and protected tree, after years of over-farming and clear-cutting. The tree produces an annual fruit crop and it is this delicious morsel that attracts legions of local goats to hop up into the boughs and pick them out. The animals stand on the dubious limbs and get down to their seasonal feast. Far from just a single ambitious goat climbing a single tree, the animals tend to swarm into the branches en-masse. Apparently, local farmers condone and even cultivate this bizarre feeding practice, keeping the goats away from the trees while the fruits mature. There is also, apparently, a secondary benefit to the goats' habits, which is found in their droppings. After they finish eating, they pass valuable clumps of the seeds, which are then pressed, to create the much sought after Argan oil. Perhaps seeing this spectacle should have been one for the Bucket List … it was definitely a "first" and I will certainly never look at Argan oil the same way again.

Arriving at the airport for the second time, we were definitely ready to go home. In more ways than one, it had been a memorable trip to this diverse and fascinating country. Thanks for the inspiration Pete. I hope you had a good laugh at our expense. I'm sure you were watching our exploits.

Chapter Nine

(26th April 2015)

Serve food at a soup kitchen

I'm not sure why I had the urge to do this, although, when I mention it to people, "Oh I'd like to do that" is often their response. I guess it's just an opportunity to do something good, for someone less fortunate, with no real reward apart from the satisfaction of doing it. I'd looked into serving food at soup kitchens locally but they all seemed to want a regular commitment, which is no bad thing but unfortunately, doesn't fit with our lifestyle (rather decadently swanning around the place ticking things off Bucket Lists, etc.) and I would hate to let people down.

My sister, Marcia, goes to the Whitechapel Mission in London three or four times a year with her church, Holy Trinity in Cookham, so I asked if I could tag along too. She said she couldn't see why not and put my name down for a shift. The night before we were due at Whitechapel I stayed at Marcia's, as we had to be up at 4am but I was SO excited I could hardly sleep.

The Mission call what we were doing the Breakfast Challenge;

"Preparing and cooking breakfast for as many as three hundred people. The breakfasts then need to be served to people who are, in the main, very grateful for your efforts and may have not eaten since breakfast the day

before, giving the opportunity to meet people from the streets in a positive and meaningful way".

We had to be at Whitechapel by 5.45am, for jobs to be allocated, with food preparation starting at 6am. The team who run the Mission are absolutely amazing and such fun to be around. Marcia lined us up for the buttered bread and toast duty, which may not seem much but for three hundred people that is a LOT of bread and butter and a LOT of buttered toast. However, with the radio turned up, we were soon dancing away, buttering endless loaves of hot and cold bread, in time with the music, while the rest of the team cooked bacon, sausages, beans, tomatoes, eggs, mushrooms and hash browns. Then we had to set up, ready for serving, which began at 8am. Cereals were lined up on the side and the hot food was put into warm serving trolleys, ready for the shutters to go up.

Those that could afford it, would pay a nominal amount per item and could choose exactly what they wanted, whereas those that had no money could get a basic breakfast for free. Bread and butter and toast were free, as was tea, coffee and hot chocolate, which would be made freshly to order. As I said before, I am more of a "people person" (rather than a "frying a few hundred eggs person"), so the customer facing role was ideal for me. Marcia and I were serving food, a lady from the mission was on the till and the people who were there doing community service were on hot drinks. You had to add up as you went along, giving the total to the lady taking cash. As the price for each item was in units of five or ten pence, it didn't appear too challenging but as the shutters went up, the enormity of the job hit home.

On this particular Sunday, it was really busy. The day centre opens at 6am because as well as food, people have access to washing and toilet facilities, plus clothing if they need it. This means there is always a rush at 8am and today was no exception. You also have to remember that some of these people are really hungry, so want their food as quickly as possible. Talk about testing your mental maths. Even though the numbers you were adding up weren't difficult, you had to be fast because the next person was already giving you their order. I have to say, the majority of the people I met were polite, courteous and very grateful that I had given my time to serve them breakfast, which was a hugely humbling experience and not what I'd expected at all. The stereotypes I had in my mind were people with alcohol or drug dependencies, bitter about their circumstances, or angry at people like me who were, quite clearly, more privileged than them. How wrong could I be. Once the rush had died down, I had a little more time to actually chat to some of them. It is a sobering thought that, in reality, any of us could be just a step or two away from their situations. All it takes is a failed marriage or job, which could lead to financial difficulty and losing your home. Once you have no home, it is hard to find work and without work you don't have the money for a home. What are your prospects when you are caught in that vicious cycle? I don't know what the solution is. I guess there isn't one really, otherwise somebody would have done something about it before now but thank goodness there are places like the Whitechapel Mission, who offer such amazing support, as best they can.

I have to say, it has opened my eyes and I view homeless people rather differently now. Not that I've ignored them in the past. There are several people living on the streets in our local town and I guess I just have "Talk to me" written across my forehead, as I do seem to attract some of the more "unconventional" ones.

For example, one day I'd taken my lunch into the grounds of the museum, to enjoy in the sunshine. I found an empty bench and sat down to eat. On the next bench were a couple of gentlemen, one quite young and the other considerably older. The older one was preoccupied with a bottle of cider but the younger of the two called across, to me to ask the time. As I told him, he said "You've got a lovely smile", which sounds a bit corny I know but he was a good twenty years younger than me, so I thought it was rather sweet. "Thank you" I replied, which was obviously my cue for him to start up a conversation, that went something like this;

Him: Wow, you're so polite too. People like you aren't normally very respectful to people like me.
Me: That's awful. I'm really sorry about that.
Him: You seem like a really nice person. Can I ask you something?
Me: Of course.
Him: Can I guess how old are you? ... a bit left field I thought but I've got nothing to hide.
Me: Certainly.
Him: I think you're ... forty-six.

Me: *That's exactly how old I am!* ... because I was then!
Him: *Really? That's amazing. You mean I actually guessed your age right? Do you mind if I come and shake your hand?* ... again, an unusual request but he seemed nice enough.
Me: *Certainly.* With that he came over and bent down to shake my hand.
Him: *Wow, you've got lovely eyes too.* ... OK, he's obviously turning on the charm, this could get a bit awkward.
Him: *Can I ask you something else please?* ... uh oh, what now? My obvious answer to this one is "No!" but that wasn't what came out of my mouth.
Me: *Of course.* ... sometimes I'm my own worst enemy!
Him: *Do you colour your hair?* ... I'm blonde with "natural" highlights (aka plenty of grey).
Me: *No, I don't.*
Him: *That's awesome. When I'm your age, I hope I meet someone like you. A woman that doesn't care about having grey hair and wrinkles.* ... and it had all been going so well!!!

He then proceeded to tell me his story, about how his girlfriend had taken all his money and thrown him out, even though he'd never been horrible to her. He'd slept on friends' couches and floors for a while but could never get a good night's sleep, so had been late for work a couple of times and got the sack. With no fixed address and no references, he was finding it hard to get a job. It was hard to sleep properly living rough, as you always had to look out for people beating you up or robbing you. He'd have to hide his belongings at night and wait for the public conveniences to open in the morning, so he could have a wash and a shave, in case the opportunity for work came up. It was a sorry tale and a classic example of how people end up on the streets. He apologised for taking up so much of my time, wished me well and returned to his friend on the bench. Such a polite young man. From time to time I'd see him around town. He would always say hello and ask me how I'd been. Then one day he just disappeared. I really hope it worked out for him but I'm not sure how realistic that wish is.

Then there was Mrs Itchy Knickers (as I called her). She approached me one day, when I was walking through town, minding my own business.

Her: Excuse me, can you help me?
Me: Of course. ... here I go again!
Her: My bottom is really itchy. ... she says, scratching her bottom. What was I supposed to say to that?
Me: I'm sorry to hear that. Have you been to see your doctor?
Her: I don't have a doctor.
Me: Oh!
Her: Can you have a look at it to see what you think? ... how am I going to get out of this one?
Me: I'm not a nurse, so I really wouldn't be any help to you I'm afraid. ... nice side-swerve I thought.
Her: What do you think I should do about it?
Me: Why not speak to the pharmacist and ask if they can give you some cream for it?
Her: Do you think they could help me?
Me: Yes, I do.

Her: OK, I'll try that then. ... and off she shuffled without a backwards glance. Phew, that was a lucky escape!

I often see Mrs Itchy Knickers around. She's still scratching and looks at me as if she thinks she knows me. I don't enter into further conversation with her, which I know sounds awful but I just don't know how to handle the situation. In fact one day, when we'd popped into town, I suddenly dragged Mr C rather violently into a shop. "What's going on?" he asked. "It's Mrs Itchy Knickers, cover me!" I replied, as I ducked out of sight. Does that make me a bad person? I hope not.

Anyway, I've digressed yet again. Back to Whitechapel. The toast had run out, serving had finished and the shutters on the food counter were down, so it was time to either wash up or help with the hot drinks. I chose the latter, as I thought I could serve people a lot faster than the Community Service young lady currently on the urn, who just seemed to be going through the motions because she had to be there. She was so slow, the crowd were growing restless. I made teas and coffees and handed out toiletries, talking to as many people as I could, until it was time to close that section down too. I can't begin to explain what a rewarding experience it was. I guess that's why the staff there are always smiling, although I think you have to be a pretty special kind of person to do that day in day out. I certainly take my hat off to them. I've done a few more stints since then, enjoying each and every one and remain constantly humbled, particularly when people recognise me and thank me for giving up my time yet again.

Chapter Ten

(1st - 3rd May 2015)

Plan celebrations for Josh's 18th and my 50th Birthdays

For a very confident and opinionated young man, trying to get Josh to make a decision is sometimes painful. His eighteenth birthday was a prime example. I'd tried pinning him down on numerous occasions, without success. "Do you want a party?" I'd asked him, "I'll think about it" was his response. Then one day he said "Mum, what I would really like is a joint party to celebrate my eighteenth and your fiftieth. I'd like to go back to Skern Lodge for the weekend, like we did for Dad's fortieth".

Well, that certainly wasn't what I was expecting ... but I liked the idea. We'd had such a good time there seven years ago. Skern Lodge is an outdoor activity centre in North Devon. The accommodation is basic but the activities suit all ages and abilities. In fact, at the time of writing, my Dad still holds the record for the oldest person to do their zip wire, which he did in 2009 aged eighty-six! Mum tried to take the record off him when we went back in 2015 but at a mere eighty-two, she was unable to steal his crown. Oh dear, I'm jumping ahead a little, let's backtrack again.

I liked Josh's idea and thought this could be another one for the List. Invitations went out and plans were made. Sadly, Dad's health was failing and he really wasn't well enough to join us this time but he was insistent we took Mum so, with reluctance (that we were leaving him at home, not reluctance that we were taking Mum), we agreed. Most people were arriving on the Friday night, so we set off on Friday afternoon, driving down with the Butler family, to make sure we'd be there to meet them. As there were nine of us, we decided to do a boys' car and a girls' car, enabling the boys to play Pub Cricket (where you take it in turns to count the legs of the pub names as you pass them, for example The Buccaneer would count as two, whilst the Queen's Head would count as zero) and the girls could just chat about girlie things, without annoying the boys. We stopped en-route for a lovely lunch at the Red Lion in Babcary (somebody got four points for that one), arriving at Skern Lodge by late afternoon. We had a bit of a social in the bar that night, before the fun and games started in earnest the following day.

There were over fifty of us, with ages ranging from three to eighty-two. Some people knew nearly everybody and some knew hardly anybody but as soon as the team building started on the Saturday morning (no pencil rolls this time), it really didn't matter. We put ourselves into groups of eight or so, then chose which activities we wanted to take part in. There are assault courses, high ropes, climbing walls, archery, underground tunnels and of course ... the zip wire. There is also a heated outdoor pool, which is just the BEST thing to jump into at the end of the day. Everyone had such a good time. You could do as much or as little as you wanted to, the emphasis was on having fun and boy did we have fun.

All meals were included and on the Saturday evening, we had exclusive use of the restaurant for a fabulous gala dinner. Once everyone had finished eating, we pushed the tables back and DJ Kevvy Kev (aka Mr C) hit the decks, keeping us boogieing all night long. It was brilliant to see all the generations having such a good time together and I had a lump in my throat watching our group of teens, most of whom have known each other from birth, having fun and being so relaxed in each other's company. They may not see each other very often these days but when they are reunited, there's none of the awkwardness so often associated with that age group. It certainly made us proud to see what a thoroughly delightful group of young people they have grown into. We danced into the wee small hours, to an eclectic mix of tunes that suited everybody, although the award for best dancers had to go to Sam and Sara who, despite the age gap (sorry Sara), were totally in sync and when they both hit the floor to do the caterpillar together, the crowd went wild.

There were a few sore heads on the Sunday morning and what better way to blow away the cobwebs than some fun and games in the pool, followed by ... surfing! Admittedly not everyone signed up for the surfing. It wasn't compulsory. Others enjoyed a walk across the golf course, down to the sea, or just chatting and catching up with friends. Sunday's lunch was a pre-prepared picnic, so that people who were travelling home had food to take with them. Not everybody set off at lunchtime, some stayed until later and others booked the extra night at Skern with us, as Monday was a Bank Holiday.

Together with a group of the late-leavers and stayers, we decided to take our packed lunches down to the shore, where we wrote messages with pebbles in the sand, did a bit of beach combing and rock pooling ... and one person was getting some "inspiration" but you'll have to read on to find out more about that.

It really was a fantastic way to celebrate two birthday milestones. Well done Josh for making such a great decision ... eventually!!!

Chapter Eleven
(7th June 2015)
Kayak from Christchurch to Ringwood

We love our kayaking! For me, it started when I was living in Bournemouth, in the eighties, where I learnt to paddle with the Lifeguards. Not during the summer, that would be far too sensible but at the end of the season, when the sea was rough and cold. My boyfriend at the time thought it would be fun for me to learn, so he bought me a wetsuit and put me in a canoe. One of our early outings was to Christchurch harbour. I was happily paddling around, when someone shouted, "Whatever you do, don't panic, it won't hurt you!", which, of course, didn't make me panic at all! I looked all around … nothing. Then I looked down … and there I was, inches above a basking shark that must have been about twenty-five feet long. Oh, if only I'd had a Bucket List back then - what an experience.

I've always enjoyed being in, on or under the water, so being out in the surf with the Lifeguards most weekends was good fun. I learnt the basics, like how to Eskimo roll, in some pretty choppy waves. The idea was, that if I could execute that manoeuvre in those conditions, I could do it anywhere. When they thought I was "ready", they took me to Lulworth Cove, to paddle to Durdle Door. The "test" was to see how close I could safely get to the cliff, without capsizing. I think it was more a test of nerve than skill but I got pretty close and consequently earnt my paddles (if that's the canoeing equivalent of wings). It's a journey I repeated, many years later, with Mr C and Josh. We'd bought ourselves a two and a half seater, sit-on-top, Ocean Kayak as a family Christmas present ... so that we could have QFT in the sea.

QFT (Quality Family Time) is a thing I put in place to make sure that, at least once a week, we would all do something together. Not necessarily big things. Sometimes it would be something like ten pin bowling, or a trip to the cinema, sometimes it would just be a fish and chip supper but somebody had to choose an activity, every week, to make sure that we actually took time out to interact with each other. Josh would sometimes groan at my insistence on QFT when he'd obviously much rather be spending time with his friends. Or he'd choose the shortest thing he could think of in an attempt to pacify me and enable him to get on with the rest of his life. Although I have to say, he often instigates QFT himself these days when he comes home for a visit. The other thing I insisted he did as a teenager was cook tea. In a bid to prepare him for self-sufficiency, he had to cook a family meal once a week to earn his pocket money. If he did, he would be paid twenty pounds at the end of the month. If circumstances (at my discretion) dictated that wasn't possible, he would still get paid but if the meal didn't get cooked because he didn't want to, or couldn't be bothered, then I docked his "wages" by five pounds per meal missed. What a harsh mother! It paid off though as he's not a bad cook these days. Sorry, I've digressed again.

Back to our first kayak, which was great while Josh was still small enough to sit in the middle seat. As he grew, we bought a second, single kayak so we could all paddle together. Josh loved it (not). Having said that, he enjoyed kayaking, he just didn't enjoy some of the paddling marathons we instigated. Mr C and I were much more enthusiastic but unfortunately, not so good at doing our research. One weekend, we thought it would be an exciting adventure for the three of us to paddle from Lulworth Cove to Durdle Door, camp on the beach for the night and paddle back in the morning. Perhaps that would convince Josh just how much fun our outings could be.

Packing minimal camping equipment into dry bags, we set off for Lulworth. We parked up and checked the pay and display machine, to see if there were any overnight charges. My eye was drawn to the sign that said NO OVERNIGHT CAMPING ON THE BEACH. "Don't worry about that" said Mr C "people camp on the beach all the time", which is true but I'm not very good at knowingly breaking the rules. Still, we'd come all this way and it was supposed to be an adventure.

We launched the kayaks and started paddling towards Durdle Door. I can't remember now just how long it took us to paddle that far but Josh was pretty fed up by the time we got there. We beached the kayaks and he promptly stormed off in a huff, as an expression of his displeasure, that didn't put me in the best of spirits, which subsequently made Mr C grumpy. So much for QFT! Tension was running high, it was getting cold and we couldn't really find anywhere out of the wind, which was picking up a bit, to pitch the tent. Our mood was darkening, as was the sky and I was beginning to get really jittery about staying. With the weather getting worse and night approaching fast, we had to make a decision. Should we stay or go? Coupled with the "no camping" rules, my nerve broke and we decided, under the circumstances, to abandon our plans and head back.

The waves were getting bigger and launching into the surf was going to prove tricky. I took the two-seater, putting Josh in the front, with me in the back and Mr C pushed us off. As he propelled us away from the shore, a large wave was forming in front of us. "I'm out of here!" said Josh and he promptly bailed out, just as the crest of the wave caught the (now very light) bow, leaving me sitting in the (now very heavy) stern. I didn't stand a chance. A tumbling mess of kayak, luggage and a grumpy, very wet, Mum (uttering words that are unprintable) tumbled back onto the beach. Josh was unhappy and I was unimpressed.

After a little bit of argy-bargy and negotiation, our second attempt at launching was more successful and at last we were off. By the time we were almost halfway back, the waves were enormous but as the wind and tide were with us, thrusting us towards Lulworth Cove, we were way past the point of no return. Josh, being upfront, was pretty oblivious to the potential dangers, whereas Mr C and I were paddling alongside each other, in total silence, exchanging anxious glances, concentrating hard on just remaining upright. Well, I say alongside each other. We were certainly in line with each other but because the waves were so big, we couldn't always see each other. I have to say it was pretty scary and although we all had life jackets and whistles (not that there was anyone around to hear those), it made me feel (sadly not for the first time and probably not for the last) a totally irresponsible parent. We saw the entrance to Lulworth Cove ahead of us but the current was now so strong that we knew we'd only have one go at getting our approach right. If we got too close to the cliff before we turned in, the backwash from the waves might capsize us but if we stayed too far out, we could leave ourselves too much paddling to do to get to the mouth of the inlet and if we missed, we certainly wouldn't get a second chance. We got as close to the cliff as we thought we safely could, then we held our breath and did the kayak equivalent of a handbrake-turn. Amazingly we made it and incredibly, as soon as we turned the corner into the Cove, it was as calm as a millpond. "That was fun wasn't it?" said Josh. Mr C and I said nothing.

Sometime later, we bought Mr C an inflatable kayak for his birthday, for those times when we were camping and wanted to "travel light" in Ruby, rather than towing Daisy, our agricultural trailer (yes really). Ruby has a very fragile (old), pop-top roof, meaning it is physically impossible to put a rigid kayak on her. The only option to transport our rugged beasts was to buy a trailer. However, kayak trailers are ridiculously expensive and because we wanted something that would hold all our kayaking equipment, together with all our other camping and weekend toys; awning, boogie boards, etc, the only option was to fashion our own. I trawled eBay for trailers and was thrilled to find one that I thought would be a good "fixer-upper". It was an old agricultural trailer which, probably for the past decade or two, had only been used to transport straw and horse feed on private land. I couldn't believe my luck when my bid won, although I'm not convinced anybody was bidding against me and the guy seemed ecstatic to have sold it! He delivered it to us and was inquisitive to find out what we wanted it for. I showed him Ruby and the kayaks and explained our plans. He laughed as he drove off, saying something along the lines of "Good luck with that one" but we were undeterred.

On closer inspection, it was huge ... and very agricultural, with a slightly rusty frame and enormous, almost tractor-like, wheels. Mr C and I stood scratching our heads, wondering where exactly to begin. We did a lot of that for quite a while before the project got underway. We decided to build a large storage area on the base that would be substantial enough to take the weight of kayaks on top. It needed to be reasonably waterproof but building the whole thing with marine ply would prove costly, so we used a mixture of materials and waterproofing - varnish outside, vinyl tiles inside, seals on the seams ... that sort of thing. It developed into a project and a half. Bemused neighbours watched as the work was carried out. "What is it?" they asked as the massive, box-like structure took shape. When we told them (and they finished laughing) they said, "We thought you were building a coffin", making me wonder if our completed venture would end up looking like some sort of rustic hearse.

Of course, there was a solution for that - decorate it to match Ruby. I painted the whole thing pillar box red, made a large flower stencil out of acetate sheets and stencilled big yellow flowers all over her. She looked much less like a coffin on wheels now ... although you could probably get at least two bodies in her, maybe even three at a push. Of course, as with all our vehicles, she had to have a name, so she was christened Daisy. She was a great work-horse and served us well, even though by the time you'd attached her to Ruby's tow-bar and put the kayaks on the top (which hung over the rear of the trailer quite a bit, in fact, we had to attach fluorescent straps so people knew just how much), the whole campervan-trailer-kayak combination was about two hundred feet end to end. OK, that may be a slight exaggeration but we were pretty long. On the plus side, you couldn't miss us! On reflection, it probably would have been more cost effective to buy a traditional kayak trailer but where's the fun in that?

Daisy was practical for long-haul expeditions but not ideal if we wanted to pop out for a quick paddle or go camping just for the weekend. Hence the purchase of an inflatable kayak, whose maiden voyage was from Mudeford to Christchurch, which is a really pretty stretch of water. We enjoyed it so much that we thought it would be a really nice idea to do the next bit of the Stour, from Christchurch to Ringwood ... although, for one reason or another, we'd never got around to it. Another one for the Bucket List then. We decided a perfect opportunity would be on our way back from a weekend of wild camping in Dorset (and polishing our plaque on Swanage Pier). As usual, we didn't do any homework. How hard could it be? We regularly cross the Stour when we drive through Ringwood, so we knew where we were aiming for. We put in at Christchurch and started paddling upstream. What we didn't realise was that, just under the

Iford bridge, there is a weir which is impassable. What we also didn't realise, was that the river at Ringwood is actually the Avon ... so we were, in fact, paddling up the wrong river, or at least not the one we thought we were on. If only something like a map had been invented, so we could plan our route before we set off. Still, it WAS a paddle heading inland from Christchurch and we were on the river that we'd INTENDED to be on, albeit with a different name, it would just never have got us to Ringwood. As I didn't know this when we set off and because we had the right intentions and starting point, I'm going to claim it for my List anyway.

Chapter Twelve
(11th - 15th June 2015)

Go to the Isle of Wight Festival

We've been to the Isle of Wight Festival numerous times before. We even took Josh when he was fourteen, as an introduction to music festivals. Sadly, that year the rain set in and didn't stop, so I vowed never to go again. Subsequently we missed a couple of years but memories fade with time and rose-tinted glasses are a wonderful thing, so it wasn't long before we got back into the habit of going again. Now I know this isn't something "new" but it is a special event for us, as Mr C proposed to me when Coldplay were headlining in 2006, so we really had to go in the year I was fifty.

The previous year had been fantastic and we'd made friends with some great people who'd pitched their tents close to ours, including a lovely couple, who we knew only as Tourette's and Burney. We called her Tourette's due to a particularly loud conversation (complete with expletives), that she thought she was having privately with her boyfriend one night. As a camping virgin, she didn't realise that people can hear everything that goes on in a tent, particularly when you are camping somewhere where you are so close your guy ropes overlap ... such as a music Festival! We called him Burney because he got VERY sunburnt. We weren't being disrespectful, these weren't names that we whispered behind their backs, it was what we called them to their faces and they happily answered to. At festivals it is perfectly acceptable to spend a lot of time with people you get on really well with without ever actually knowing their real names.

Oh and that was the year we met Anna, which actually was her real name. She's another one who, as she stumbled past, saw the invisible writing on my forehead that reads "Talk to me". We'd not long put our tent up and were sitting out in the sun with a glass of wine (we're posh festival goers we are), when Anna pitched up next to us. Well, I say pitched ... she didn't actually have a tent, just a bag of clothes and an airbed (which she'd thrown in at the last minute as an afterthought). In fact, she hadn't actually planned to go to the Isle of Wight Festival at all but her benefits cheque turned up the day before so, on the spur of the moment, she bought a ticket and here she was. She'd had a hard life, at least that's how it looked, with her own sad story to tell ... which she told us in the first few minutes of her arrival. Anyway, she parked her stuff next to ours and asked where she could get water. We pointed out the location of the drinking tap and she started searching around on the ground. Assuming she'd lost something, we asked what it was she was looking for. "An empty bottle I can use for water" came the reply! Taking pity on her, we offered her a glass of wine instead. The trouble was, we only had two glasses. Not a problem, she scoured the ground again, found an empty can, shook it to make sure there were no cigarette ends in it, then held it out saying "This will do" as she smiled and gestured for us to pour wine into it (very classy). She was an interesting character our Anna. I say our Anna because we sort of adopted her, well looked out for her anyway. We never actually saw her in the arena, although she assured us, she had listened to some of the bands … not that she could remember which ones. At night, she would curl up on her airbed, next to our tent. People stumbling back in the early hours would wake us with cries of "Oh my god, there's a dead body", to which we would respond "Don't worry, it's Anna, she's just sleeping". Strangely, whenever that happened, they never managed to wake Anna up.

All in all, it was a fab festival. The weather was glorious and we sort of teamed up and had great fun with Tourette's and Burney. Unfortunately, they didn't get to see the headliners on the Sunday as, due to work commitments the following day, they had to leave early. We'd said our farewells earlier in the evening but when we returned to our tent that night, they'd left a very touching note (sophisticatedly scribbled on the back of a burger box) which read *"Lovely meeting you - safe trip home & see you next year! Burney & Emma"*

Sadly, even with the wonders of social media, we were unable to trace them … there are a lot of people called Emma out there and we had no idea what Burney's real name was. Somewhat surprisingly, we didn't exchange details with Anna either. In fact, she was still asleep on her airbed as we decamped and left. For all I know she could still be there now.

Knowing Bucket List year was going to be an expensive one, I decided to save a bit of money by booking Early Bird tickets for the festival. To save even more money, I used my NUS Student Discount card, reducing the cost of my ticket even further. It meant we had to collect the tickets on arrival, rather than receiving them by post but it all seemed pretty straight forward and I thought it would be well worth it for the saving I'd made. However, what I'd saved on my ticket, I'd more than blown on our transport to the Isle of Wight, booking seats on a rib. It's by far the quickest and most exciting way to cross the Solent. Also, it takes you right up the Medina and drops you just a short walk from the Festival site. We'd chosen one of the earlier crossings that would get us there in plenty of time to set up before the music began on the Thursday night.

Once at the site, we found the booth for collecting Student tickets. "Wait over there and you'll be escorted to the main entrance to pick them up" the girl said, gesturing towards a group of teens-to-twenties students, sprawled across the grass. We didn't really look like we belonged with them, nevertheless we joined the group and waited ... and waited ... and eventually, someone came to lead us all through the site to the ticket office. Once there we queued, again, to get our tickets and wristbands. It all took so long, I was beginning to wonder if saving those extra few pounds had been worth it. Eventually, wristbands attached, we were officially in.

We were hoping to pitch in the same spot as the previous year but this year, that particular part of the field had become "Respect Camping", which meant you had to keep the noise down after 10pm. That was certainly not for us. You'd have had to pre-register to camp there anyway, so we made our way to the next area, where we were met by a surly steward saying, "Purple Camping is full". How could it be full? The Festival site had only been open a few hours and most people don't generally arrive until the following day, when the main stage opens. "You'll have to go to Yellow Camping" he said, pointing back down the hill, towards the original student waiting area, where we'd started. I was not impressed but we had no choice. We retraced our steps until we saw a large, grassy area with a big sign in the middle saying "Yellow Camping". With only a dozen or so groups dotted around the field, we could take our pick of where to pitch. We chose a central location, not too close to the loos but not too far away either, on the edge of the camping line, so we'd be able to find our way back relatively easily at night and within striking distance of the refreshment van, for our morning cuppa and bacon butty. Perfect.

We got out our camping chairs and had started unpacking the tent, when another steward came rushing over. "I'm sorry, you can't pitch here" she said. "Why not?" I asked, "The guy at the top said we had to come to Yellow Camping". "I know" she said, "but this is Yellow Overflow Camping". "Show me the word Overflow on that sign" I said rather abruptly. "I'm sorry," she said, "it hasn't been signposted properly but I can't let you pitch here until Yellow Camping is full". "Well, we'll sit here and wait for Yellow Camping to fill up then" I said, even more abruptly. "I'm really sorry but I can't let you do that either, my job is to keep people moving on. You'll have to go to Yellow Camping over there" she said, gesturing at a gap in the hedge, even further down the hill. I was beginning to lose my sense of humour but it wasn't fair to take it out on her, it wasn't her fault. Huffily, we repacked our stuff and made our way to the gap in the hedge, where we met a third steward. "Is this Yellow Camping?" I asked. "Yes" said the sheepish young lad. "Great, we'll find a spot here then" I said, somewhat relieved. "I'm sorry," he said, "but you'll have to move into the next field, this part of Yellow Camping is full". In utter disbelief I looked around and glimpsed a spot, big enough for our little Force Ten tent and right on the edge of the camping line, just the way we like it. I held eye contact with the young lad whilst pointing at the spot that I'd spied and said, in my most authoritative voice, "I am going to pitch my tent right there and you are NOT going to stop me". "OK" he said, his face flushing bright red as he promptly looked in the opposite direction. I was still muttering about the injustice of it all as we started putting the tent up. I glanced across at the girl sitting outside her tent, directly opposite us, on the other side of the firebreak pathway. She nervously smiled, then got up and ran away. Great, she'd obviously heard me asserting myself with the young steward and taken flight. How to impress your neighbours! We continued erecting the tent and finally managed to unpack the rest of our stuff.

Eventually the job was done and we could relax in our camping chairs. We were about to sit down when we glanced across at our nervous neighbour. This time, she sat there grinning from ear to ear and this time she had a chap next to her, who had the same Cheshire cat expression. Unbelievably, it was Tourette's and Burney from the year before! Apparently, she'd been saying to him how she wished we'd exchanged details and asking if he thought they'd bump into us again this year, to which his response had been that in a crowd of sixty-thousand people it was highly unlikely. Yet here we were, right opposite each other ... what are the chances of that? If it hadn't been for my student ticket and getting moved on (twice), we may never have met up. Some things are just meant to be. We found out their real names, socialised all weekend, swapped phone numbers and subsequently kept in touch. In fact, we've become great friends with Tourette's and Burney, or should I say Emma and Nathan. For some bizarre reason, I'd kept the note they'd left for us the previous year and much to their amusement, I showed it to them when they came over for dinner one evening. They asked if we'd appreciated the remainder of their special brew that they'd put inside our tent, as a leaving gift ... but unsurprisingly we hadn't! Somebody must have seen them stash it there and snaffled it away before we got back that night. You never know, it may even have been Anna!

We've had some good times together since then. Why they want to hang out with us old crusties I do not know, I'm only a year younger than Emma's Mum but whatever the reason, we're glad they do. However, that is not the only coincidence involving Emma ... as you will find out.

Chapter Thirteen

(20th June 2015)

Attend the Summer Solstice at Stonehenge

I've always been a bit of a hippie at heart. I love the clothes and the flowers and for almost as long as I can remember, I've wanted to go to the Summer Solstice at Stonehenge. My brother used to go and said it was great. When I lived in Somerset I had a boyfriend that went. I asked him if he'd take me but he said I was too young! I don't suppose my Mum and Dad would have let me anyway. This was the boyfriend who had a Ford Cortina with a whippy aerial and as was fashionable at the time, a sun strip across the top of the windscreen that you could stick letters on, which were generally used to add names above the driver's and passenger's seat. His used to read "Guy 'n' Becky", then when we started going out, he removed Becky's name. Sadly, he didn't replace it with mine, so we used to drive around with it just saying "Guy 'n'   "! I wonder if you can still get them. How cool that would look on Ruby's windscreen!

Ruby, in case I haven't said so before, is a proper hippie van, covered in flowers inside and out, full of bunting, bells and crochet. She was PERFECT for taking to the Summer Solstice. We'd talked about going when we were with Emma and Nathan the previous weekend. "You could always park at mine and walk" Emma said, explaining that the roads were likely to be at a standstill. Believe it or not, she only lived a couple of miles from Stonehenge. You see, we really were destined to meet again. We thanked her for her offer and said we would use that as our backup plan, if we couldn't get any closer. As it happens, we did manage to get closer, much closer. Admittedly we'd had to sit in traffic on the A303 for a while but that had given me time to get out and collect ox-eye daisies from the side of the road to make a garland for my hair (as a replacement for the artificial flower garland I was wearing already ... oh yes, I was dressed for the occasion).

We actually arrived at the Visitor Centre around 6pm, an hour or so after the gates opened. It's very organised these days, with ample parking and we managed to get a good spot. It was early evening so, once we'd parked up, we cooked tea, then thought we'd take a wander down to the henge because for the solstice celebrations, you are allowed right up to the stones. When I lived in Reading, as a child, we had a school trip to Stonehenge and in those days we were allowed to clamber all over these incredible monoliths. These days, visitors are kept at a distance, with a definite "no touch" policy and accessibility only allowed during solstices.

We were a little surprised how commercialised everything was. There were food and beverage stalls, retail outlets, even entertainment for the children ... and more portable loos than there were at the Isle of Wight Festival (or so it seemed). However, once you'd got past that bit, the walk to the stones themselves was a tranquil bimble along a grassy path, which felt much more at one with nature. There were lots of people around and the ambience was amazing. You could get in and around the stones with ease and although it sounds a bit corny, when you hugged the stones (which, of course, I did) where they'd been bathed in sunlight all day they felt warm and somehow alive. It was magical though, as if you were touching thousands of years of history.

Lots of people had settled in for the duration but as we had visitors arriving at our house the following day, we decided the best thing to do was to go back and have a bit of a kip in Ruby, returning in the early hours of the morning for the dawn spectacle. When we did return, a few hours later, we immersed ourselves in the stones once again. The atmosphere was really beginning to swell as the air was filled with drumming, chanting and a general feeling of happiness. It was hypnotic. Eventually, we stepped away from the main circle and found ourselves a spot to view the sunrise. The people-watching was fascinating. Such a random collection of human beings gathered together in anticipation.

As usual, my invisible sign shone through and we were soon deep in conversation with a gentleman called James, who felt compelled to tell us his life history although, by his own admission, his chatter was rather chemically enhanced. He was a fascinating and very interesting chap, who insisted we took his details (which I did) and keep in touch (which I have). I liked him, he was quirky. Luckily, we managed to stop him talking just in time to witness the dawn and although I am not religious, in any way, I feel compelled to use the word "spiritual" when describing the moment. It was very special.

As the sun rose high in the sky, we walked back to Ruby with a real sense of peace. As a celebratory meal, we treated ourselves to breakfast from one of the refreshment stalls, then climbed back into bed, to grab a bit more sleep and avoid the queues of traffic leaving the car park. When we woke up, the majority of the vehicles had left and we managed to drive straight out, although by now I was in need of a good cup of tea … and I knew just where to get one. Thanks Emma, that was one of the best cups of tea ever.

Chapters Fourteen & Fifteen

(27th June 2015)

Visit 50 pubs in Gosport (past and present)

&

(27th June 2015)

Own an original piece of Art

Here we go then, another entry on my Bucket List from my so-called friends! In the past, we've had some marvellous nights out in Gosport with Deb and Colin. We always set off with great ambitions about the number of pubs we are going to visit but sometimes things distract us. Like the night we met Andy Beetlestone. It all started when, a few years ago, we'd been to a House Gig where Jesse Terry, an American Folk singer/songwriter, had performed in a friend's flat, to about thirty people. We didn't know any of his songs but I, in particular, love Folk music (the inner hippie in me coming out yet again, plus events from my childhood, which we'll come to later). It was such an intimate gig and he chatted about himself and his songs along the way, which made it really personal. At this point in time Passenger, a young (by our standards) musician from Brighton called Mike Rosenberg, had just had his first chart success. I'd followed him since he started out and would watch him perform whenever I could. He wasn't a really commercial artist, remaining true to his roots by continuing to busk and do smaller gigs. I wondered if he'd do a REALLY small gig at ours. Where's the harm in asking? So, I messaged him;

Hi Mike

Had an amazing evening at a Private House Gig last night by an American guy called Jesse Terry at the end of his European Tour. We told him about you, so he may well check you out. Really enjoyed seeing you, as always, at The Brook last Wednesday and know you love your busking but if you fancy testing the waters with a House Gig at ours message me. It's an awesome experience if you haven't tried it yet.

Best wishes

Lesley

Being the genuinely nice guy he is, he replied;

Great. Thanks so much Lesley. I would love to but at the moment it's just bonkers (having achieved international success, topping the charts in many countries around the world, with all the media attention which that attracted) ... *maybe one day. Thanks so much for the support xx*

I'd realised he'd be super busy but you never know, maybe one day he'll look me up! A month later, we were on a night out with Deb and Colin and popped into the Kings Head, where Andy Beetlestone was playing. We enjoy pretty much any kind of live music but tonight, he was playing covers of a wide range of popular songs, so we were really into it. It was just him on guitar and his friend on a Cajon box drum. They were brilliant and soon had people dancing on the tables … including me! We were enjoying it so much, that we stopped crawling and settled for this pub. He paused for a break and I called him over. "That was fantastic. Have you ever done a House Gig before?" I asked. "I played in somebody's house once. We were booked for a birthday but they put us in the corner of an L shaped room and we ended up being background music. That's about it." he replied. In for a penny, in for a pound … "Would you like to come and play at ours? You won't be stuck in a corner and people will actually be there to listen to you". He said he was interested, so we exchanged details, suggested a couple of dates and agreed to be in touch. A few days later, with a slightly clearer head, contact was made and the date was set.

Something else you need to know at this point is that, at the beginning of the year, Mr C and I had started playing the guitar. My brother, Frank, had recommended a good beginner's guitar, so we bought two and started downloading tabs from the internet, to teach ourselves. Every day we would practice in our conservatory, much to Josh's horror as his bedroom was just above.

One song we really liked and could play in a pretty recognisable fashion was Opposites by Biffy Clyro, which gave me another idea. Andy popped over to discuss the final details of the gig and I asked if Mr C and I could do a number with him. He was up for it. I told him which song we'd like to do but he said he wasn't familiar with it. Mr C typed the title into iTunes and played Biffy's version but Andy shook his head, saying he still didn't recognise it. Unfazed, he asked for the dog-eared sheet of A4 containing our tabs. He looked at it for a minute, picked up my guitar … and just played it … beautifully! We were in awe. It had taken us months to master the basic strumming, now here he was, totally unacquainted with this soft-rock melody, yet adding all the twiddly bits (a technical term that probably only those amongst you who are accomplished guitarists will understand) and sounding like he'd been playing it all his life. I didn't even realise my guitar could produce music like that. "Yeah, that should work" he said casually. This gig was turning into a musical extravaganza for our oh-so lucky friends!

The big night arrived. Andy came over early to set up and we did a bit of a run-through together. We'd decided to have our five minutes of fame at the start of his second set, so he could warm people up for us first. Pushing the furniture back, we filled our conservatory with bean bags and cushions, setting Andy up in the bay window. People arrived and after a few drinks and nibbles we got started. He was AWESOME. Everyone was singing along, clapping and cheering. Andy chatted a little bit about himself and the songs he was playing. He said he'd never performed this way before but he was a natural at it. After an hour or so, he took a break. Our friends knew we'd been teaching ourselves the guitar but we hadn't let on about our surprise debut. Just as Andy was about to resume, Gordon said "Aren't you two going to play something for us then?". What a perfect introduction, I couldn't have planned it any better myself. "Well, as it happens" I said with a smile "for one night and one night only, supported by the fabulous Mr Andy Beetlestone, I give you ... Mr and Mrs C" and with that, we picked up our guitars and joined him on the imaginary stage. To be fair, we were pretty awful but Andy kept it all together and the crowd went wild! The evening had been everything I'd hoped for, in more ways than one and I think everyone enjoyed it, although maybe not quite as much as us. Sadly, we haven't played our guitars much since then. I guess we peaked at the height of our fame. One day we'll get back into them. They still sit in the corner, gathering dust, reminding us that they are there (our guitars of course, not our House Gig guests).

So that was the result of one of our mini pub crawls. Now it was time for the big one - the fifty pubs of Gosport. Deb and Colin had researched a route, trying out bits of it in preparation. There aren't actually fifty pubs that are still open in central Gosport. Quite a few have been turned into shops and houses but many of those still bear the signs that they were once such establishments, so they would count. I bought us all shot glass necklaces, stylish ones with purple beads and a big fifty on the receptacle. The idea was, if we reached a stage where we didn't want a whole drink, we could buy one between us and share it in our shot glasses. We picked Debbi and Morgan up and went over to Deb and Colin's for a 10am start. Deb had made us party bags, containing things like pork scratchings, tissues and hand gel - all the essentials. They poured us a drink, "one for the road" before we got going and ushered us into the lounge. Hanging on the wall was one of Colin's oil paintings. He's a fantastic artist and we keep pushing him to make a career out of it but at the moment, he just paints for pleasure. This one was a large canvas of a beautiful beach and seascape. "Wow, that looks like the beach at Skern Lodge" I said. "Do you think so?" he replied. We all admired it and agreed that it looked just like it. "Good" he said "That's what I was hoping you'd say because that's what it's meant to be. Happy Birthday". How amazing! My own, unique piece of artwork produced by a very dear friend. It now hangs in pride of place in my lounge and every time I look at it, takes me straight back to that lovely beach and great weekend.

Still a little speechless, although not for long, I handed out the shot glasses and it was time to head off on our challenge. The weather couldn't have been better, blue skies and sunshine with a gentle cooling breeze. Morgan was chief photographer and his job, with the aid of his mini tripod (you can make your own jokes up there), was to take a picture of us outside every pub, as evidence of our challenge. The first pub wasn't a pub anymore, so it was a quick snap then onwards. The second hadn't opened yet but we couldn't wait, as we were on a mission, so after the obligatory photo, we carried on.

I'm not sure which part was more fun that day, going into the pubs and explaining to the landlords and patrons what we were trying to achieve, or the hilarity of getting a group photo outside each establishment. Sometimes, to get the right shot, Morgan would set up the camera, using the timer, on the other side of the road, dashing back to take his place in the group. We'd all keep our fingers crossed, willing it not to go off just as a car was passing. When it worked you could probably hear our cheers reverberating around the whole of Gosport. I checked us in on Facebook at every pub, so that friends, who were following our exploits, could see how we were getting on and Kath, who was joining us later, would know where to find us. All the people we met were so friendly and supportive and towards the end the bar staff really didn't mind that they were only serving two drinks to seven people, they just liked being involved. With the finish line in sight, Mr C took charge and hurried us along because we the clock was against us. Luckily, we made it to our last pub, the Jolly Roger, just before they called time. We all sat down with a sigh. Believe it or not, what we really wanted was a drink but not just "A drink", we wanted our own drink, one that we could choose for ourselves, rather than having to share a communal beer or cider. We'd walked almost nineteen miles, which had taken us ten hours and forty-five minutes ... but we visited all fifty pubs, past and present. Impressive eh?

Chapters Sixteen & Seventeen

(11th July 2015)

Take part in a Run or Dye event

&

(11th July 2015)

Change the colour of your hair

I love colour. I've always loved colour. My house is full of colour, from the walls to the soft furnishings and my Mum always said I'd never have any dress sense as I always insisted on wearing clashing colours as a child. So, when I heard about the Run or Dye events, I knew they had my name written all over them. Run or Dye is a five-kilometre run, inspired by the ancient Hindu festival of Holi, known as the Festival of Colours. You run, or walk, through five dye zones, turning into, what the website refers to as "a technicolour canvas of fun".

I signed us up as a team of five; Fi, Debbi, Maisie, Kath and myself, for the Kings Park run, in Bournemouth. You get issued with an official number, a white t-shirt bearing the run or dye logo and your own packet of powdered dye. The object is to get covered with as much paint, in as many different colours, as possible. Maisie had done a bit of research and bought us all sparkly headbands, to keep our hair off our faces and different coloured sunglasses, to protect our eyes from the powder. Equally thoughtfully, although not quite so tastefully, Fi had bought us all white leggings. White leggings? Does anybody look good in white leggings? I can answer that question … no they don't! They do make a great canvas for the paint though.

We arrived in plenty of time and collected our goody bags, supplied by the event organisers, from the registration tent. The whole thing starts properly with a musical warm up, led by a very enthusiastic compere on stage, whose job is to whip everyone up into a frenzy, before unleashing them into the park. During this frenetic beginning, you are encouraged to start throwing your packets of dye over your fellow participants. Once a suitable state of hype and base colour have been achieved, everyone makes their way to the start line, ready to be released in waves. Each dye station you pass through, along the route, is a different colour and the aim, really, is to run through these as slowly as possible, to get covered by as much powder as possible. We were like children playing in a rainbow. At the end, everyone congregates back at the stage for more musical mayhem and of course, more paint. Who'd have thought you could get so excited about powder paint? We were smothered from head to toe and my blonde hair was psychedelic.

Back at the car we removed our headbands and glasses, leaving our faces with stencilled accessories. Once we'd stopped pointing at each other and laughing, we talked about what we were going to do next. We hadn't bothered taking a change of clothes because we knew this stuff wasn't coming off without a hot shower. Fortunately, our car has leather seats which we could wipe clean, so that wasn't going to be a problem.

However, it was now early afternoon and we hadn't had any lunch. The trouble was, where could we go for lunch looking like this? Like the car, it had to have wipe clean seats. Luckily, just down the road was a Burger King - perfect (under the circumstances) and as it was close to the Run or Dye venue there were bound to be lots of people in a similar situation. There weren't! Nevertheless, once through the door, we were committed ... and hungry! We went to the counter to place our order, as if it was the sort of thing people looking like us did every day. However, from the reaction we got from the staff and our fellow diners, you'd think we were aliens from outer space. Didn't they know what had been going on right on their doorstep that morning? Obviously not!

Conveniently "change the colour of your hair" was another challenge on my List. My friend Pam thought this would be fun. Pam and I met when I started gliding, at the Portsmouth Naval Gliding Centre, where her first husband Chris, an experienced glider pilot, took me under his wing (excuse the pun). Neither Pam nor Steve were into gliding but they were supportive partners and our friendship, as a foursome, evolved away from the airfield. When Josh came along, he and Pam (a natural with young people, as her status in Girlguiding and the relationship she has with her stepchildren and their families testifies) developed a very special bond. He loved our visits to see her at work and over the years, Pam got him involved in lots of promotional work at the Shopping Centres she managed; opening a museum, dressing as a clown to assist a children's entertainer and even taking part in a fashion show. As he got older, he loved it when I would drop him off on his own so that he could take Pam out for coffee, making him feel very grown-up. In turn, whenever the circus came to town, she would take him along to one of the performances, as her special treat. She has also been his voice of reason over the years, always there to listen, providing him with sound, unbiased advice. Without a faith of our own, Steve and I decided not to have Josh christened, leaving him to make his own choices regarding belief when he was old enough. However, Pam has been the closest thing to a godparent he could have and if there was a job description for the role, she would certainly fulfil every aspect of the criteria. Pam is married to Joe now, who Josh looks up to in equal measure. He still makes time for coffee with them (when he's home) and they continue to follow his (and our) various exploits with a keen interest.

Showing Pam my photos, after the Run or Dye event, I asked if this counted as changing the colour of my hair. "Absolutely" was her reply. Great, that's two challenges ticked off in one day then.

Chapter Eighteen
(14th July 2015)

Pack your bags and set off with no fixed agenda

Oh yes, we could do this one, no problem. Once again this called for Ruby, our trusty steed. We love the idea of catching a ferry then, with the freedom of an open road, travelling around until something catches our eye that we think we need to stop and investigate. We'd taken her to Ireland a few years back. A brilliant week of wild camping, which Ireland is fantastic for, touring around the Dingle Peninsula and the Ring of Kerry, sleeping on the beach and catching our own fish supper. The original plan was to fish for our supper most days and we did try but Mr C is not, shall we say, a proficient piscator. Not having fished since he was a young lad, he enlisted the help of Morgan, a seasoned rod and tackle man, to give him a lesson before we left. So, although we fished for our supper most days, we only actually caught something to eat once. We'd lost quite a few lures during our early attempts, so had to pop into a fishing tackle shop for some more ammo. We took advice from the proprietor, as to where would be a good fishing spot and when the tide would be right. Subsequently, later that afternoon, we spent quite a while on our recommended harbour wall, losing a few more lures amongst the rocks, with not even so much as a nibble.

"That'll do for today" said Mr C, not overly disheartened, as he enjoyed practicing his casting. "Try once more for luck" I said, urging him on. To pacify me, he did and as he made his final fling, I called out "Be lucky Mr C". Almost straight away he could feel tension on the line. This wasn't unusual as he'd got snagged on so many things before but this time, there was movement. "I think I've got something!" he said and we both squealed with delight. We weren't actually sure what to do next, as we'd never got this far before. Carefully he started reeling in and yes, we could see there was most definitely a fish attached and coming our way. Looking like a pro, he lifted it out of the water and landed it on the harbour wall.

It was a good-sized sea bass (we'd studied, in detail, the fish recognition posters displayed at the various fishing spots we'd tried previously) and I LOVE sea bass. "Quick, get me a stick or something, I don't want it to suffer" he said. Frantically I looked around and found a piece of wood. I handed it to him and he clonked the fish on the head ... at which point I promptly burst into tears! I am such a softie. I mean, I'm realistic about where our food comes from, don't forget I did Rural Science at school and worked at livestock shows but I'm not very good with the actual "mechanics" of it all. If you put a fish on a plate in front of me, head, tail, the works, that's absolutely fine but I would NOT be able to eat at one of those restaurants where you have to select your fish from a display tank, where they're still swimming around. Once it's dead, that's fine but if I've made eye contact with it before it died, I couldn't eat it knowing that I was the one responsible for its death. Silly I know but that's me. However, self-imposed rules are just a guideline and after all Mr C's efforts there was no way I was going to miss out on eating this one … once I'd stopped sobbing and apologising to it.

We took a photo of our prized catch, to show Morgan. Excited by the fact that we'd actually caught our own supper we returned to Ruby, trophy in hand. We got out the chopping board and the biggest knife we could find and Mr C set to work removing its head and tail and gutting it. At this point, Bertie Bass started moving. Now, I know that fish, like chicken, have muscle memory but this was REALLY moving. I mean, it was jumping around so much that, at one point, it actually jumped off the chopping board. "Are you sure it's dead?" I asked, rather stupidly. Mr C just looked at me, in a pitying fashion, saying "It's got no head and no organs, I think we can safely say it's dead". I think, if his hands hadn't been covered with scales and guts, he'd have patted me on the head at that point. I did video the last bit of its death throes and when we showed it to Morgan, on our return, he agreed that he'd actually never seen a dead fish move quite that much before.

Fish prepped and flattened out like a butterflied chicken breast (we had to try to get it pretty flat as we've only got a little grill for it to fit under and we we'd forgotten to book ourselves onto Morgan's advanced fish filleting course), we put it on the grill pan, ready to cook. What to have with it though? Again, as this was uncharted territory for us and we hadn't considered putting suitable accompaniments in Ruby's store cupboard. We headed off in search of a shop but it was now early evening and everything was closed. Well, this was rural Ireland. We found a petrol station that was open which, luckily, sold a few groceries. We ended up with a tin of peas and a tin of potatoes – true sophistication. Unfortunately, the tin opener broke as soon as we'd opened the peas. We tried everything to get into the potatoes but just didn't have the tools for the job. We had equipment to make holes big enough to drain the water out but not big enough to get the potatoes out. Admitting defeat, we ended up with just fish and peas ... but it tasted great! When we reached somewhere we could get a signal on our phones, we sent Morgan the picture of our catch. "Nice Pollock" was his reply. Well, at least now we know we like the taste of Pollock too!

So, that was Ireland and as I've said already, we'd also taken Ruby over to France, using only the Aires de Service and wild camping spots. This had worked really well and there was still plenty of France to explore, so we thought we'd give it another go. We bought cheap tickets for the Newhaven to Dieppe crossing and set off ... with no fixed agenda. On the ferry, we flicked through our Lonely Planet guidebook, pondering whether to turn left or right when we disembarked. We chose to go right and head for the D-Day beaches, which I'd visited on a school trip but Mr C had never seen. We stopped at each of the beaches and did some of the museums, which proved both fascinating and very moving. We even spent a couple of nights camped on the beaches, which was lovely but somehow felt oddly disrespectful. Silly really because life goes on and they are, in fact, holiday resorts now. We also found the cemeteries very sobering but it felt good to pay our respects. With so much to see and a restricted timescale, we knew we couldn't do it all, so chose the things that were of particular interest. As a glider pilot, I found Pegasus Bridge especially fascinating and the skills of the glider infantry almost incomprehensible. I'm glad stories like these are preserved for the generations to come, so many of them are absolutely incredible.

Our adventure took us via the Bayeux Tapestry, as far west as Le Mont-St-Michel, which is stunningly beautiful. After walking across the causeway, in a sweltering thirty-two degrees, we had the most expensive beer we've ever bought … but boy was it worth it. Watching the speed with which the tide comes in, around the island, was spectacular.

There was so much more we could have seen and done but time was against us (this was a VERY busy year). However, on our way back to the ferry, we decided we could squeeze in a quick detour south of Caen, to drop in on some old friends of mine, Chris and Denise, who I hadn't seen for years. Chris had served in the Royal Navy with Steve and subsequently lived and worked in the Middle East but had a French property, which was now their main residence. We'd tried to match up with them when we were camping in France many years ago but our timings weren't conducive to a meeting. This time I'd checked they were going to be around and was determined to make it happen. We spent a lovely day with them and as we were preparing to leave, we agreed that we should make the effort to catch up when they were back in the UK, as they often came over for short visits. "We've got a mobile home over there, that we use as a base" they said. "Fantastic" I replied, "Give me your address and we'll come and see you when you're over".

They gave me their address ... it's a mile and a half from our house! So, we'd driven halfway through France (well, not quite but you know what I mean) to see them, when we could have walked to our local pub to meet up for a pint.

My diary entry at the end of our expedition read *"Trip Statistics - 8 days, 819 miles, €40 camping fees, 50 cents on tolls (+ €6.30 to cross the Pont de Normandie but it was worth it), £170 on fuel (but we came home with a full tank), £200 on eating out (but you can never have too many moules) and the 44 litres of wine purchased to bring home (I didn't count what we consumed while there). Total spending £740 + ferry fare of £146"* and all achieved without any fixed agenda.

Chapter Nineteen

(23rd July 2015)

Get a log burner installed

We've always wanted a real fire but our reasonably modern property doesn't lend itself to housing one. We'd started looking at log burners, thinking if you can put one in a lighthouse, surely you can put one in an ordinary house but our lounge just wasn't suitable. We were very envious when Maggie and John announced they were having one fitted. Maggie was bubbling with excitement and not just because of her log burner. "You should go and look at the showroom" she said, "You can have them fitted in conservatories these days". My face lit up. We love our conservatory, it is the social hub of our house, as it's the biggest room we have and we practically live in it. It's open plan, accessed from both the kitchen and the dining room, with big comfy sofas and a glass table and chairs, where we sit to eat our family meals and impromptu suppers. Remember, it was big enough to accommodate thirty people and a musician for our House Gig and it is party central when it comes to family gatherings, themed dinner parties and New Year Celebrations. We love the layout and didn't want to change anything around, however, there was one small piece of wall where a log burner might just fit and if it did, it would be the focal point of the room.

Out delivering leaflets for Mr C's business one day, we found ourselves next to the showroom Maggie and John had talked about, so called in to speak to, as it turned out, the guy who had fitted theirs. We really didn't have a lot of space but we knew you could get some very small log burners because we'd met Dan and Paula on one of our wild camping trips near Swanage and they have a log burner in their campervan! After looking at the traditional log burners, explaining what we were trying to achieve, the chap nodded knowingly and said, "I think I have just the thing you're looking for". He showed us a more modern range of log burners, including a semi-circular one, with glass on three sides, which could be wall mounted. It looked perfect. We arranged for his surveyor to come out to check its viability and kept our fingers crossed.

When the surveyor visited, he said he'd never installed one in a set up like ours before but saw no reason why it wouldn't work. We had to do a few things in preparation, like having fireboard fitted on the surrounding walls and replacing our wooden floor with slate. It was all systems go. The day after the Fifty Pubs of Gosport pub crawl, we ripped the floor up and by the middle of the week the fireboard was up and plastered (I still haven't got around to painting it, you know me - a starter not a finisher) and the slate was down. We were ready. Installation took place the day after we got back from our trip to France and we were thrilled ... it looked gorgeous. Fellow log burner owners, Debbi and Morgan, came over to admire it. The men made fire and we decided on an impromptu supper in honour of its inaugural lighting, finishing with a dessert of ice-cream, topped with blackcurrants preserved in alcohol, a homemade gift from Denise, courtesy of the harvest from her French garden. A fitting celebration for a beautiful addition to our home.

Chapter Twenty
(24th July 2015)

Get Maizie Restored

Maizie is my Mazda MX5 and I love her. I bought her in 1993 after my previous car, Gertie Hyper-speed, died. It was the early nineties and we were DINKYs (dual income no kids yet). Looking for a replacement, my criteria was; sports car, two seats, no roof and red. Steve was a sucker for research and set to it. MX5s were still relatively new to the UK, as Mazda had only started importing them three years before, which meant the price of a brand new one was pretty steep. I said I'd be happy with second hand and after a bit of hunting around, he found a blue one in a dealership fairly locally, suggesting I take it for a test drive to see if I liked it, having never driven a sports car before. The arrangements were made and I was VERY excited. We were allowed to take it out on our own, well it's a bit difficult to get three people in an MX5 and after I'd driven it around for a while, I was getting more confident with the handling, cornering, etc. Steve suggested he had a go too. "OK, let's see what it can really do" he said almost burning rubber as we pulled away. He wasn't a dangerous driver but he drove faster than me and knew how to handle a car. I felt like a co-driver in a rally as we tore around the country lanes, putting it through its paces. "I like it" he said, "I think you'd have a lot of fun in an MX5. We'll look around for a red one for you". He looked at me and I turned on the puppy eyes … "But I like THIS one" I whispered. "I thought you wanted a red one" he said. "I thought I did too but she's such a pretty blue … I think I've fallen in love with her" I said sheepishly. "I wish you'd told me that before I thrashed the pants off it" was his response but by the time we got back to the dealership he realised he was fighting a losing battle, so went into negotiation mode (he could drive a hard bargain) and I knew Maizie was going to be mine!

It was a similar story with Ruby really. She was "conceived" in a traffic jam in France, in the days when we used to take camping holidays in the Vendee with Craig and Caroline. "I'd love a VW campervan" I'd told Mr C, as we sat in stationary traffic and to pass the time, we started thinking about the practicalities and viability. By the time the traffic was moving again, we'd both agreed it was a good idea and I'd decided I was going to make a start, by crocheting a blanket for her … well, it's important to begin with the basics. Back in the UK, we read reviews and scoured the internet. Although the traditional Split screens and Bays look lovely, they are small, expensive and notorious for breaking down. With the next generation, the T25 or Wedge, you get a lot more for your money and a much bigger van. A T25 was within our price range, so we started looking at some and having a few test drives, to see what our options were. One particular weekend we took a trip to Bournemouth, where we'd made arrangements to view a few. The second one we looked at was Ruby. Mr C took her for a spin and I just sat in the back … grinning. He looked at me in the rear-view mirror and sighed a knowing sigh. When we got back to the chap's home, we told him we were very interested but that we still had a couple to look at and would let him know by the end of the day, as we knew somebody else was due to be viewing her. "She's the one" I said as we drove off and even he had to agree, she was. By the end of the day, we'd paid a deposit and made arrangements to collect her. Again, I think it was fate that brought her into our lives. She came from one of my hometowns and the chap that owned her was one of the chefs at Coriander, our absolute favourite restaurant in Bournemouth (sadly now closed). I just love coincidences.

Back to Maizie. She was my pride and joy and I loved every minute that I drove her. When I bought her, Mum and Dad were living in Spain but kept a base in the UK, not far from where we lived, which I kept an eye on when they were away. As it happens, it was in the same cul-de-sac where Debbi and Morgan were living (yet another coincidence)! We didn't know each other very well in those days but as there still weren't that many MX5s on the road, they would recognise me and wave when I popped over. Debbi was pregnant at the time. I remember Mum telling me the baby had been born, a little girl and they'd named her … Maisie! Of course, we're great friends now but I always tease Maisie that she was named after my car because my Maizie was here first. When I was pregnant, I worried that I would have to get rid of her (my Maizie, not Debbi's Maisie) because that's why her previous registered keeper had sold her, even though she hadn't owned her that long. "Wait and see" Steve had said, very sensibly, although I did have one scary moment. At my first booking-in appointment at the Maternity Hospital, the doctor examined me and said, "I think it may be twins", to which my immediate response was "I can't possibly have twins, I've only got a two-seater car". He raised his eyebrows, probably thinking I shouldn't have even contemplated conceiving if I was that shallow. I was whisked off for a quick scan. "Don't worry, there's only one baby in there but it's a big one" he said. What a relief! In preparation for my "big baby" (he was only eight pounds nine ounces actually), I started gathering equipment. I didn't really want a pram because a lot of modern pushchairs were suitable for new-borns and would last me considerably longer. Most new Mums buy a pushchair based on colour, style or brand. Not me. I took Maizie over to a shop in Portsmouth, parked in their car park and said, "If you can find a pushchair that I can use from birth and fits in the boot of my car I'll buy it". Challenge accepted, they brought about half a dozen down to the car and tried them all. One fitted …. I bought it. Forced car sale crisis averted, Josh was the coolest baby on the block, cruising around with the roof down in his stage-one car seat.

We did have a sensible family car, that we could all fit in, too … if you call an XR4i a sensible family car (although when she went to the scrapyard in the sky she was replaced with a much more practical four-door BMW). When Steve was terminally ill, he gave me two instructions and asked me to promise that I'd carry them out. 1) As soon as he died, I was to book a holiday for six months' time because by then he said I'd need it and be ready for it. 2) I was not to change anything of any significance for the first year, then review my situation, making any decisions that needed to be made when things wouldn't be so emotionally charged. He was so practical it was sickening but I did what he said and it was wise counsel indeed. True to my word, I did book a holiday, in fact I booked two, for Josh and I and by the time we went away he was right, we both needed it. Also, I didn't make any major changes in our lives for the first year, including cars. Steve's car, Bertha, was a big 7 Series BMW and I, of course, still had Maizie. Bertha was obviously the more practical car for me, with a five-year-old son and his friends, who needed ferrying here, there and everywhere but I heeded Steve's words and rather than selling Maizie, I took her off the road for the winter. Benefactor Bob came down and put her into hibernation in the garage. When my year was up, I had to make a decision about which car to keep. Bob came down and put Maizie back on the road for me, making sure everything was OK as she was an old lady of sixteen by now, so that I could decide what to do with her and which car to keep. I put the roof down and took her for a blast along the motorway, to the New Forest and back, a huge grin on my face the whole way. It was like being reunited with an old friend and she was such a joy to drive. I told Bob my dilemma, who just shrugged. "Keep both" he said … so I did. Over the years, she started showing her age. I'd put a new vinyl roof on her when the original had split but she had a few rust patches coming through. I had made sure I put her in for regular services though, so she was mechanically sound, it was just the cosmetics.

When Brian, Mr C's car, died we didn't replace him, he just started using Bertha for the commute to Slough each day. By the time Josh started driving, we owned three vehicles - Maizie (because I loved her), Bertha (because she was so practical and such a comfortable car for distance driving) and Ruby (our recreational vehicle).

Unfortunately, we couldn't get insurance for Josh on any of them, not that they'd be practical cars for a learner anyway. About six months before Josh's seventeenth birthday, my sister, Louise, was changing her car and offered him her old one, which was ideal as a first car. Phil the Fiesta joined the family and we were now a three-person household, owning four cars. Josh loved Phil but once he'd passed his test, he wasn't quite as gentle with him as he should have been. Poor Phil encountered a catastrophic failure, when his head gasket went. We'd called out the RAC and as luck would have it, the engineer on duty turned out to be a friend of ours. Ken said it was unlikely that the repair would be cost effective but relayed him to our local garage, for them to confirm. Sadly, it was indeed the end of the line for Phil, so we left him with our mechanic while we decided what to do with him (Phil not Josh). By now, Josh was commuting to college and work and I'd got used to the fact that I'd been absolved of taxi duties. He needed a new set of wheels, pronto. Enter, stage left, Emma the Punto. She was cheap and cheerful, as there was no point in spending too much because Josh was hoping to go to Uni in a few months' time. A couple of weeks later, coming off the motorway, he heard a terrible noise and saw a plume of smoke. He pulled over and called the RAC. When the engineer (not Ken this time) took a look, he shook his head and said, "Your head gaskets gone mate". Josh looked at him in horror "My Mum's going to kill me, I've only just blown the head gasket on my last car". The engineer assured Josh that he couldn't have done that much damage in such a short space of time, so it must have been on its way out when we bought it. He had her towed home and we parked her on the drive, while we decided what to do with her too. Of course, now we were a three-person household, owning five cars.

We were in a bit of a dilemma. We didn't want to throw more money at a cheap car again but was it worth spending money on a good one that Josh only needed for, what was hopefully going to be, a very short time now? We drew up a list of pros and cons and finally decided we'd buy a reasonably priced trade-in as, by now, Mr C was no longer commuting and had been thinking about a more practical, around-town car for his KC The Gadget Man business. Welcome Harvey the Hyundai. The little i10 was perfect and in the interim, Josh would just have to car share. All these events happened in such quick succession, we had suddenly become a three-person household, owning a total of six cars! It was time to rationalise. We donated Phil to the college where I worked, for the students to learn on and we sold Emma to a chap who was looking for a "project". By the time Josh went off to Uni, we'd reduced, slightly, to a two-person household, with just four cars. This was much more sensible, even though, if I'm honest, we're not really "car people".

Shortly after Emma's "incident", Maizie had started overheating. I dropped her off with our mechanic (who still had Phil in his yard, waiting to be collected at this point), to take a look. He phoned me up with his diagnosis. "Bad news I'm afraid, your head gasket's gone". Are you kidding me? Three head gaskets in as many months! How can that even be a thing? I contacted Doctor MX5 who, perhaps not unsurprisingly, only works on MX5s and is thankfully fairly local. He told me to fill the radiator, put the heater on full blast and drive her over so he could take a look. He confirmed the head gasket had indeed gone but other than that, he thought she looked pretty sound and with a bit of welding she'd probably be worth restoring. I looked at Mr C. Once again, he raised his eyebrows "Go on then" he said and I just smiled.

She was at the Doctor's for quite a while in the end but it didn't matter, I had plenty of other cars to drive. When we went to collect her, she looked beautiful. My diary entry for that day read *"Maizie comes home - Look who's had some restoration work done! So excited to be reunited with my beloved Maizie Mazda. We've been together for twenty-two years now and I handed her over to Doctor MX5 who has done a complete overhaul on her and she looks GORGEOUS. After driving around in Ruby for the past couple of months (which I have loved) it is good to be back on the open road in my baby; power steering (such luxury), a steering wheel which is about eighteen inches wide rather than eighteen feet, a gear stick which is three inches rather than three feet long, a snappy little gear box rather than one that feels like I'm stirring a bowl of porridge and as close to the road as a skateboard rather than a bus ... I feel like I'm in a Formula 1 car! Even though it's raining cats and dogs I drove her home with a HUGE smile on my face."*

I probably should have had her restored ages ago but it seemed fitting that I had it done in my Bucket List year.

Four days later, Kath and I were on the train, coming back from a day trip to London, when I got a text message from Mr C which read;

"You are not going to be happy. Your lovely restored car now has a damaged rear bumper. I was in Titchfield seeing a client and as I was reversing into a space a woman with kids in the back decided to cut across. We hit and the rear plastic bumper is badly discoloured. She blamed me and I her but I have a witness that said my reversing lights came on as I reversed and she went for the gap and missed. Anyway, I have her address but I don't know if it is worth going through the insurance. The bumper is physically OK. Just needs a respray. Sorry but I don't think it was my fault. Typical that it happens to your newly restored car. xxx"

I groaned. "What's happened?" asked Kath. "It's Maizie, she's been in an accident" I replied. "Oh no, poor Maizie ... but she's only just got back from the doctors" said Kath. By now, we were aware that everyone in our very busy carriage had gone quiet. "Maizie's my car" I explained out loud and everyone breathed a sigh of relief. "What happened?" asked Kath, so I read the text message, with everyone still listening in. There were sharp intakes of breath from our fellow passengers and one chap piped up "I wouldn't want to be your husband when you get home". I started to explain that I knew it was only a car and I was grateful that nobody was hurt but I loved that car, she was my baby. By now people were sympathetically leaning over seats and across the aisle. I showed them the pictures of her, looking beautiful after her restoration work and they all cooed as if she was indeed a real baby. "I've even written about her in my diary" I said and I read them the entry (above). Although I was feeling a little emotional, we all had a bit of a laugh and it was certainly a talking point for the rest of the journey. In fact, it got everybody in the carriage talking, which is a rarity in this day and age, so it was nice that something good had come out of this unfortunate incident. Luckily, the damage was only superficial and after another quick trip to the Doctor's, she was back to her full glory.

Chapter Twenty-One
(1st August 2015)
Go to the Sidmouth Folk Festival

My maternal grandparents were originally from Cookham but retired to Devon when I was five. They purchased the old Station Master's House in Sidmouth, which was at the end of a branch line that had closed just two or three years before. It was a fascinating building, situated high above the town, three-quarters of a mile from the seafront. Apparently, the railway track ended here to deter day-trippers who, it was felt, would lower the tone of the town. I always like to drive past when we're in the area and it still looks very much like a station house. Some of the original station buildings also remain, although they are used commercially these days by builder's merchants and the like. I loved every inch of that house, probably because I loved my grandparents and therefore loved everything associated with them but possibly because it was a bit quirky, like me. Indulge me as I take another trip down memory lane and describe it to you.

Isn't it strange how powerful childhood memories can be and how they never seem to fade with time, even though you can struggle to recall what you did last week? I remember every room in that house, each one seeming very square. I don't mean square instead of round, like our room at the Belle Tout lighthouse, I mean square rather than oblong, as most rooms in modern houses seem to be. I'm not sure if this actually was the case but that's how I saw it as a child and with very high ceilings it gave the illusion of each room being almost cuboid, which always fascinated me for some reason. The sitting room was at the front of the house and was originally the Station Master's living room where, apparently, Queen Victoria once sat while she waited for her train. It is well documented that she and her family loved Sidmouth, so it's more than likely that's a true story. It was a dual aspect formal room that didn't get used very much, probably because it wasn't worth heating it when it was just my grandparents there. Not that they were formal people, it was just that it was a big house and it was an extra room that they didn't really need to use too often. When we did sit in there it always felt like a special occasion, even if it wasn't and I would drink my cup of tea, which was ALWAYS in a bone china cup and saucer, sticking my little finger out, pretending to be royalty.

In the hallway, under the stairs, was a toilet. A big room compared to your average under-stairs loo, probably because of the length and height of the stairs. It was a modern addition to the house but for some reason my grandmother gave it an old-fashioned twist. I have no idea why (and I never actually asked her) but she would always put Izal toilet paper in there. Remember the sort? It was like greaseproof paper but with even less absorbency. The only thing I ever used it as was tracing paper and it was great for that. She did provide ordinary loo rolls as well, for "those that preferred it" although I can't imagine why you would ever choose to use the crunchy stuff.

Opposite was the door which led to the other living room, which was the one they used every day. Originally this had been the waiting room but it now served as a lounge/diner with a dark wood, barley twist, gateleg table and chairs, two wing-backed armchairs facing the fire and a small TV in the corner. When visiting on my own, of an evening my grandparents would sit in the armchairs to watch Crossroads and Coronation Street, which we NEVER watched at home, while I sat at the dining room table drawing (sometimes using that multipurpose toilet paper). The fire would crackle gently in the hearth and the room would be filled with the sweet smell of my Grandfather's ready rubbed tobacco.

A second door from this living room led to the kitchen, a relatively small internal room that was once the ticket office. What would have been the counter was now a window which looked out into the vestibule. The vestibule itself was accessed internally, from the third door in the living room, or externally from what my Grandparents used as the back door. It was a long, narrow room with whitewashed brick walls and a stone or tiled floor, which meant you could come in from the beach or the garden without having to worry about taking your shoes off. I adored the vestibule for lots of reasons. Firstly, it housed my collection of buckets, spades, fishing nets and of course all the treasures you could collect from the beach using these tools. Secondly, at the far end, by the kitchen (ticket office) was the original station toilet, still with the authentic brass "penny in the slot" toilet door lock, which my Grandmother would polish until you could see your face in it. Not only was the lock still on the door but you still had to pay a penny to get in! Decimalisation had recently taken place but on the outside of the kitchen windowsill was a pot of big old brass pennies and although it could get pretty chilly out there, the novelty of using this lavatory never wore off. The third reason I adored the vestibule was because next to the toilet, opposite the ticket office, were sheds (now rooms) which, back in the day, had been used for storing wood and coal but now housed my Grandfather's workshops (and were probably one of the reasons they bought this rambling property in the first place). My Grandfather was a Silversmith and although he had retired commercially, he would still make things for the family and a few specially commissioned pieces. I remember one of his commissions was for a friend who, for some reason which I can't recollect, had lost a finger. These were the days of early prosthetics and the gentleman had a false finger made for him. My Grandfather's role in this was to manufacture a gold band, which was fixed to the finger, so that when the digit was attached (I can't remember exactly how but I seem to recall some kind of thread that it was screwed onto) the ring covered the join. How ingenious! I was fascinated by my Grandfather's skills and I'd sit for hours, watching him make things as he patiently showed me and explained the different techniques he used.

We'd often take trips into town together and as I got a little older, approaching my teenage years, I loved going into the one and only fashion shop in, what was then, a sleepy little holiday resort. It wasn't really the sort of shop you'd imagine to be frequented by an elderly gentleman but he would always humour me as I liked to look at the trendy jewellery, or pieces of "tat" as he would call them.

On one particular occasion I'd fallen in love with a necklace that was nothing more than a metal loop with a hook on each end, which would probably bring you out in an allergic reaction within the hour, with your initial hanging from it. They were all the rage and very à la mode. He looked at it with me, turning it this way and that, studying it carefully … and then we left. The next stop was our compulsory visit to the quaint, old-fashioned Mocha Tea Rooms, situated on the seafront, where tradition dictated that we would have a cup of tea (Earl Grey of course, which is probably where I developed that taste) and a piece of rich, moist fruitcake (his favourite). Suitably refreshed, he pushed his cup to one side and produced, from his pocket, a pencil and paper whereupon he proceeded to draw his interpretation of the coveted necklace, making sure I approved of the "improvements" he had made to the design and dimensions.

Returning to his workshop I watched in awe as he set about making it for me in silver (because that wouldn't bring me out in a rash). We had great discussions about the gauge of the wire, the size and font of the letter L, how to make sure it hung correctly (not like the cheap one which had the pendant loop in the wrong place and therefore dangled at a wonky angle) and how to make sure the edges of the hooks weren't sharp (like the one in the shop which would gouge chunks out of you). There was so much attention to detail and it took him ages but he was determined that I wasn't going to waste my pocket money on a "load of old junk". Placing the piece around my neck, he leant back and nodded his approval. I was now the proud owner of a very special, yet very fashionable, bespoke creation.

I really did appreciate everything he did for me but I don't think it was until I was considerably older that I realised just how lucky I had been. Like when I was into horse riding in a big way and charm bracelets were all the rage. He created a complete bracelet, from the links and the traditional heart shaped clasp with a keyhole, to each individual charm, all horse related of course; riding hat, saddle, stirrups, etc. I still treasure the things he made for me. Such a talented man and one of the gentlest men you could ever wish to meet.

Back to the Station House and the rest of the property. Upstairs had been modernised, changing one of the bedrooms into a bathroom (which at the time was the biggest bathroom I'd ever seen) and putting partition walls up to divide another large room into two bedrooms. The room I used to sleep in had a chunky, wooden framed single bed which you literally had to climb up onto it was so high. The sheets and pillowcases were candy striped flannelette and the blankets and eiderdown that topped it off weighed a ton. In winter, my Grandmother used to put hot water bottles between the sheets because with such high ceilings the bedrooms never really warmed up properly. I would get undressed as quickly as possible and dive into the pre-heated linen. Pinned beneath the hefty bedclothes, I would watch the shadows being cast by the nightlight candle, which had been lovingly placed on the bedside table, until I drifted off to sleep. However, the most fantastic thing about the upstairs was the way you could come downstairs. The staircase had a magnificent, polished, mahogany banister, which smelt of beeswax polish and felt beautiful. Although I wasn't a particularly adventurous child, I couldn't resist climbing on at the top and sliding all the way down. It was scarily high, pretty precarious and because of the dimensions of the building it was so long you could really pick up speed. Of course, I didn't ever do this when any adults were watching!

I would often ask to spend time with my Grandparents in the school holidays. Summers were the best. I'd go for walks with my Grandfather along the disused railway line, which was still home to the old train tracks. Using his walking stick (the one that I've incorporated in my wicker shopper) we'd gather blackberries from the top of the hedgerows, which I'd proudly take home to make fruit crumble with my Grandmother. Or we'd make yachts out of tin cans cut in half lengthways. We'd use putty as ballast and to secure the lollipop stick mast, to which we would attach a paper sail. Launching took place in the River Sid, one of Devon's smallest rivers, either down by The Byes or in the pool it forms before disappearing beneath the shingle beach, just as it reaches the sea at the end of the Esplanade. Simple pleasures but so much fun.

The freedom we had as children in those days would be almost incomprehensible now. Of a morning my Grandad would walk me down to the beach at Jacobs Ladder, a mile or so away down a long steep hill, armed with buckets, spades, fishing nets and towels, where he'd set me up for the day then leave me to it. He would come down on his bicycle (he never drove a car) at lunch time, under the pretence of bringing a freshly made picnic lunch but probably in reality just to check up on me. At the end of the day he would return on foot to bring me home, which usually meant loading him up like a packhorse and then asking him for a piggyback when it got to the steepest part of the hill! We'd stop on the way to pick a posy of wildflowers for my Grandmother, as she always said wildflowers were her favourite. Depositing my beachcombing treasures in the vestibule, I'd wash my hands in the thick, creamy, lather created by a bar of Pears soap and once my Grandmother was happy that I'd done the job properly, we'd take our places at the gateleg table, just in time for tea. I would repeat this process for days on end, year after year, sometimes taking school friends with me (who always loved to be invited), sometimes just making friends on the beach. Why was the weather always sunny in your childhood summer memories? It must have rained or been cold sometimes but when I look back all I remember is sunshine.

Getting back on track, slightly, another of my lasting memories of my times in Sidmouth was the annual, weeklong folk festival. There has been a folk festival in Sidmouth since 1955. The Sidmouth Folk Festival I remember is nothing like the huge, out-of-town event it is today. It started as a small dance event, showcasing international talent on a stage erected in the grounds of The Knowle, once one of the most famous houses in Sidmouth. Laying out your picnic blanket on the grassy slope you could watch national dances from countries around the world, full of intricate, colourful costumes and music that would set your toes tapping from mid-afternoon until late at night. It was an event that was revered throughout the folk world and to which people would travel from all corners of the globe, on an annual pilgrimage, to attend. In addition to the programme of events on stage, during the day the town would be filled with music and dance, including Morris Dancers with bells a jingling and pigs' bladders a flapping. I was the proud owner of lots of bells ... and I mean LOTS. I would tie them on to anything and everything; shoelaces, belts, bows in my hair ... you name it, I'd put a bell on it! Of an evening there would be live music and late-night ceilidhs in all the pubs although, sadly, I wasn't old enough to attend those. The grand finale was the Torchlight Procession. Starting at The Knowle, everyone would light their torches (which consisted of a fuel-soaked rag, stuffed into a tin can, attached to the end of a wooden staff) and follow costumed dancers and musicians in a procession down to the sea. On a given signal, we doused our torches in the waves and the firework display would commence, bringing the festival to a spectacular close.

Somehow, not long after moving to Sidmouth, my Grandparents got involved in the folk festival. It started when they were asked to help out selling tickets, which was a basic affair in those days. They would set up a little table at the entrance, taking money in a cash tin and dispensing tickets from old fashioned, sugar paper, rolls, the ones that come in various colours with little perforations between each ticket. One of my jobs would be to wind the ticket rolls back up if they accidentally rolled off the table and uncoiled onto the floor (which happened regularly). A job that made me feel very important, especially knowing how valuable these little strips of paper were. I am unsure how their involvement grew but it did and over the years they became an integral part of the organising committee, which they continued with until age and ill health forced them to stop. Sadly, when they stopped being involved, I stopped going. It wouldn't have seemed right without them somehow ... until now!

I'd been threatening to take Mr C for years but as I said earlier, it is not the event it used to be and tickets for Folk Week, as it is now known, are pretty expensive, particularly if folk isn't your favourite genre. However, it just so happened that this year we were going to be in the West Country during Folk Week. We'd booked a long weekend in a cottage in Dawlish with Debbi, Morgan, Fi and Andy. We had no real agenda, making plans as we went along. My one request was that, at some point, we visit Sidmouth. I knew I could never recreate the scenes from my childhood but I wanted a quick trip down memory lane for a flavour of how it used to be. Being the fab friends that they are, they made time to appease me. We headed straight to the seafront, parked up and went for a stroll along the prom. It didn't disappoint. Drawn by the sound of an accordion, we were soon immersed in folk culture, music and dance. As we wandered through the town there were buskers and dance troupes on every corner. It was enough to transport me, albeit temporarily, back in time to something very close to my heart. As brief as it was, I'm glad I was finally able to do something I've wanted to do for many, many years.

I can't end this (very long) chapter without one more little ditty from this laughter-filled mini-break in Devon. One day we took a train ride to Paignton, followed by a ferry trip to Torquay. The weather was hot, sunny and just perfect. After something to eat and a couple of drinks we went wandering through the pretty Pavilion Gardens, where the English Riviera Wheel is situated. This attraction is a bit like the London Eye with enclosed gondolas but MUCH smaller. Debbi and Andy decided they didn't want to go on it but Fi, Morgan, Mr C and I did. We were queueing up for tickets when the effects of the beer took hold and Mr C needed to dash off to the loo. We really fancied being in a gondola on our own, just the four of us but the operators had adopted a policy of filling each gondola with the maximum of six people each time. Approaching the lady in the ticket booth I had a moment of inspiration and seized the opportunity. "Excuse me" I said in my poshest voice, "I'd like four adult tickets please but I was wondering if it would be possible for us to have a gondola to ourselves? You see, my husband has Tourette's and I would hate him to offend anyone if we had to share". "Of course," she replied, looking slightly embarrassed as she radioed our request to the chap who was allocating people to gondolas. Mr C came bounding back, all smiles and completely oblivious. When we got to the boarding area the "embarkation operative" looked over, questioningly, at the lady in the booth. She nodded, I smiled, the four of us got on and the attendant closed the door. Bingo!

It wasn't until we were at the top of the wheel that we told Mr C what we'd done. His face was a picture. Sorry Mr C but it did make us chuckle. For "added effect"

Morgan started swinging the gondola, making us laugh louder. As we completed our first rotation, the chap who'd let us on started shouting that if Mr C didn't behave, we'd have to get off! Unfortunately, that made us laugh even more. Poor Mr C ... but it was a good prank and I think he's forgiven us.

Chapter Twenty-Two

(6th August (should have been 10th April) 2015)

Have a "Girls' Night In"

This was one chosen by my friends, the Pink Ladies and a potential victim of our extended stay in Marrakech. With the flights cancelled and the inevitable delay to our return to the UK confirmed, I had borrowed someone's phone to get a message back to my girls. As I was stranded for (what was then) an unknown length of time, I suggested they go ahead without me, thinking we'd be unable to get a refund at such short notice. As luck would have it, they took pity on our plight and we were able to transfer our booking, which meant my "Girls' Night In" could stay on the List!

We'll start, naturally, with the back story. The original Pink Ladies, you may remember, were the eight batty birds in Barcelona for my fortieth. The group sort of evolved when we purchased our hot tub. Lots of people said having a hot tub was a bit of a novelty, which would wear off. I can confirm that, for us, it hasn't. Mr C and I use it almost every day and when Josh was younger, it was a great place to actually get him to sit and talk to us, something teenagers rarely seem to do with parents these days. It was one of the things that counted as QFT.

We loved our hot tub from day one and often, when one of the girls popped in for a cup of tea, or a glass of wine, I would dig out a swimsuit for them to use and we'd take our beverages into the warm, inviting waters. Realising how often this happened, it made perfect sense for my girlfriends to have their own swimwear, which could be left at our house, for whenever they popped in unexpectedly and fancied a dip. So, we purchased a number of identical, pink, flowery swimsuits in a variety of sizes (each with a different coloured bee-shaped button, so we knew which belonged to who), together with identical, pink, flowery accessories for our hair, to keep it out of the water. It was a perfect solution, especially when we were all together of an evening for a group catch up, which was how the Pink Ladies were reborn.

In the months that followed, Fi discovered the wonders of Groupon and would find deals for Spa days, which proved ideal for Pink Ladies' days out. Of course, as we were the Pink Ladies, we HAD to wear our "uniform". On our first Spa Day together, we were quite self-conscious about being a gaggle of giggling girls, in identical costumes, with identical flowers in our hair. Somebody even once asked if we were a synchronised swimming team. A lovely thought but with no disrespect to my friends, none of us really have the body of a synchronised swimmer, so this made us giggle even more. Sadly, the costumes didn't last forever, as they rotted in the chlorine after a while. So eventually, the time came for us to bulk buy another set of identical costumes. Of course, we continued with the pink floral theme for the Pink Ladies' costumes version two.

Fast forward to the *Pink Ladies Girls' Night In*. This is a package offered by a local hotel, their advert reads as follows;

Enjoy quality time with friends, without worrying about taxis home or getting cold and wet running from restaurant to bar. Arrive at the hotel to goody bags filled with treats and spend your afternoon swimming in the pool or relaxing in the steam room, sauna and whirlpool. In the evening head to the bar for jugs of cocktails before retiring back to your room to get the slumber party started. We will deliver a selection of sharing platters, chick flicks and popcorn to your door.

What's not to like about that? There were seven of us, so we booked three rooms. Fi and Deb had shared in Barcelona, as had Kath and Jo, so they were obvious pairings, which left Caroline, Debbi and I in the room for three (a double bed and a sofa bed), obviously the bigger room, so quite clearly the one destined to be the party room. We arrived in dribs and drabs and didn't actually get as far as the spa facilities on the first night, deciding to just have fun hanging out in the room. We'd been slightly concerned that the "selection of sharing platters" included in our deal would be more like snacks and nibbles, so people had brought extra food and plenty of wine. We'd also arranged for Debbi's husband, Morgan, to deliver pizza and garlic bread later in the evening, as we weren't that far from where they lived and really didn't want to spend extra money by ordering a takeaway. We got dressed up in our robes and slippers and congregated in the party room, where we played with all the things in our goody bags - face packs, nail varnish … you get the picture. We had chosen some DVDs but didn't really watch them, as we were too busy making our own entertainment.

Back at home, Morgan had started cooking … and then the platters arrived. They were enormous! We tried calling Morgan to cancel but it was too late, he was already in the car park, waiting to hand over the contraband at the designated fire exit. We had so much food, it was ridiculous and despite some sterling efforts, we didn't really do the feast justice. I don't remember what time we went to bed that night but I do remember our faces ached from laughing so much.

The next morning, we'd agreed to meet for a leisurely breakfast, before making our way to the pool. Now, by the time we'd organised our *Girls' Night In*, we were due version three of our Pink Ladies' costumes. Sadly, it wasn't really the right time of year to purchase swimwear and we were struggling for choice. Undeterred, I'd kept searching and one night at Debbi's after one, or maybe two, glasses of wine, her daughter Maisie and I came across a swimwear sale section on the internet. Bingo! Although not pink, one particular design jumped out at us and at five pounds each I just HAD to treat my girls to them. Maisie and I were laughing, A LOT, when we placed the order but what could the girls say? They were presents after all and it would be rude of them to be ungrateful. I was so excited when I got to the Click and Collect desk a few days later. Gathering the Pink Ladies together for our Girls' Night In planning meeting, I presented them with their gifts. There were initial shrieks, followed by a little bit of hysteria. It took a good few minutes for everyone to stop laughing enough to speak. They were simple, halter-necks; plain black at the back … so far so good … but with a huge picture of a lioness's face on the front. We composed ourselves enough to put them on, then the hysterics started again. The big cat's huge, piercing, blue eyes were … let's just say, at "chest" level and her bearded chin … well, you can probably work out what level that was at! No wonder they were reduced to five pounds and it does pose the question - just who thought that this design would be a good idea?

So, in our upmarket hotel, at the *Girls' Night In,* you can imagine the childish giggles as we made our way down to the spa in our slippers and robes, covering up THOSE costumes. We'd received some odd looks when we were wearing swimsuit versions one and two in public but this unveiling topped them all. We made our way out onto the terrace, as the weather was glorious. People did not know where to look as the pride of lionesses disrobed and reclined on the sun loungers. The young waiter nearly dropped our jugs of Pimm's as he came towards us … all those eyes and beards … I bet the poor lad has had nightmares ever since! After a while, we became oblivious of what we were wearing (a bit like Linda's lovely birthday jumpers) and just got on with enjoying the rest of the day – a pride with pride! Thanks, girls, for a great couple of days and SO MANY laughs.

Chapter Twenty-Three
(28th August 2015)
Take part in a Murder Mystery

I've always fancied doing a Murder Mystery but it was another one of those things I'd never managed to get around to, once again meaning this was definitely the year to make it happen. I was planning to pressgang somebody into organising one but to my delight, a birthday present from Deb and Colin was a promise to host a Murder Mystery dinner party. How splendid!

The invitations came out;

Murder at Midnight

Captain Pigwash cordially invites you to join his table aboard The Lady Midnight on Friday 28th August 1776 at 7pm

It is the evening of 3rd July 1776 and the Lady Midnight has sailed into Boston Harbour, just in time to see the birth of a new nation.

On board are a group of emigrants from the Old World pursuing various hopes and dreams in the New World but as you gather for a celebratory meal in the Captain's cabin, one guest is missing.

The body of Lord 'Lucky' Farquhar has been found in his cabin. He has been murdered! Luckily an English constable, Michael McClue, is also on board and will help you find the killer.

Mr C you will play the part of Lord Bristol Twin-Bore An aristocrat with a reputation for a debauched lifestyle, he has been appointed Governor of New Bristol. Nobody is sure if he has genuinely turned over a new leaf!!!
Lesley you will play the part of Lady Josephine Twin-Bore
The twin sister of Lord Bristol Twin-Bore, she is accompanying him on his new posting. Like him, she has attracted a reputation for dissolute living!

You will be joined at the Captain's table by Abraham Washington (Andy) *and his wife Aretha Washington* (Fi) *and Beryl* Sheep (Deb) *the most famous actress of the time.*

It would be fun if everyone dressed up but it does not have to be authentic to the period, costumes or a few props to complement your character will be fine and can be from a different century (it's not easy finding 18th century clothing in charity shops)!

Please let me know if there is anything you do not eat, I will try to be as authentic as possible to the period in history but cannot guarantee the freshness of the food as we will have been at sea for several weeks!!

Looking forward to the evening

Captain Pigwash 🐷 and Beryl Sheep xxxx

How exciting! We started planning our costumes. Mr C's and mine were pretty obvious. We've always been ones for a bit of dressing up and went through a phase of themed dinner parties with Maggie, John, Linda, Jim, Sharon and TC. It all started with a Burns Night many, many moons ago where we were "tartaned" to within an inch of our lives. From there we progressed to St David's Day, St Patrick's Day, Oktoberfest and Trafalgar Night. Each time, the outfits would get more flamboyant. You'd never believe "grown-ups" could get so excited by a bit of lederhosen or a leprechaun costume.

It was going to be the Trafalgar Night ensemble that would serve us well for this Murder Mystery though. My outfit had been relatively easy; my pink wedding dress, hair styled in ringlets and a chunky cameo. Mr C's needed a little more work. I bought a blazer from a charity shop, cut it to make it cropped at the front, leaving it longer to fashion tails at the back. I added gold braiding, brass buttons and epaulettes (made of cardboard, gold fabric and curtain fringing) and accessorised with a red sash. That was the top half sorted, now for the bottom half. White trousers were needed to make some breeches, but I couldn't find any anywhere. Having a lightbulb moment, I decided to take Mr C shopping (and he hates shopping, particularly for clothes) for white leggings instead (and you know what I think of white leggings). We were delighted (me more so) to find a pair in the ladies' section (of course) of a reasonably priced fashion shop. They were slightly cropped and had three brass buttons at the bottom … perfect! Queueing up to pay I was holding them up against Mr C, pondering. "I think they may be a little see-through, would you like some opaque white tights to wear underneath?" I asked him. The looks we got from our fellow shoppers were hysterical ... but on the night he did wear the tights under the leggings, to protect his modesty. I made him silver foil buckles for his shoes and the most outrageously oversized bicorne hat, stiffened with wire coat hangers, to top off his white wig. His hat was so wide that if he wore it side-to-side, he couldn't fit through the door, so he had to wear it fore-and-aft when manoeuvring! To play the part of Lord Bristol Twin-Bore at our Murder Mystery night he ditched the hat but kept the wig. My Trafalgar Night costume was perfect as it was for Lady Josephine Twin-Bore.

The evening started with sea shanties and cocktails and continued with fine dining and crime solving. We laughed until we cried and the murderer was suitably named and shamed ... although I'm not going to tell you who it was, in case you ever want to host this party yourselves.

However, this wasn't the only Murder Mystery to take place within the year. For Colin's fiftieth birthday, which I shall come to a little later, eight of us headed to Cornwall for the week and each evening was themed. Now it just so happened that my birthday fell on one of the days we were away, so why not do another Murder Mystery to celebrate. The first one had been so much fun and we felt we'd got the hang of it now. Once again Deb and Colin were in charge, well they were the experts, choosing another nautical affair, only this time set in the nineteen-thirties, with eight of us aboard the RMS Olympic for some mid-Atlantic mayhem.

The Time: *1935*
The Place: *RMS Olympic, Titanic's sister-ship bound for New York.*
The Murder: *A death served up at dinner followed by a suicide! Seems cut and dried...but is it?*
The Scene: *Over the course of a dinner party you must unravel the mystery and help DI Ivor Notion solve this gruesome whodunnit! Each of your guests will play the part of one of the suspects in the case ... as you seek to unmask who it was who did the dastardly deed!*

The Suspects:
Angeline Desguys: *The daughter (Debbi)*
Eamon Etonian: *The butler (Colin)*
Irma Patsy: *The secretary (Sara)*
Esau Hytall: *The emigre (Keith)*
Toby O'Notably: *The long-lost son (Morgan)*
Dawn Trodden: *The maid (Deb)*
Edward 'Ed' Butte*: The manservant (Mr C)*
Enid Ann Hallaby: *The companion (Me)*

Everyone was in character from the word go. Deb was a very subservient maid, greeting and seating us as we arrived at the beginning of the evening. Colin and Mr C were also "in service". However, the day before we'd realised, we needed more supplies but being in the middle of nowhere, we didn't want to waste time driving for miles for such a domestic duty, we had much better things to be doing. As we'd had an on-line grocery shop delivered the day we arrived, we decided the best thing was to do another one. The only slight spanner in the works was that the only delivery slot we could have was during the evening of the Murder Mystery. Nonetheless, it was the easiest way to get our shopping, so we booked it. When the driver arrived at the door, he was met by the maid and the butler, with me close behind. As the "Lady of the house" I stood to one side, giving instructions about which of the groceries were to be taken where and by whom. The delivery chap, a little bemused, handed over the crates to each allocated "servant" as I complained bitterly about not being able to get the staff these days. He had a big smile on his face when I asked him to pose for a picture with my maid though ... and dutifully complied.

Keith and Morgan deserved Oscars for their fantastic German and Irish accents, which they maintained throughout and Colin's comedy moustache managed to navigate its way around his face to produce a myriad of expressions.

So as far as bagging entries on my Bucket List, this was definitely two for the price of one thanks to my thespian friends and a few props!

Chapter Twenty-Four

(10th September 2015)

Visit Buckingham Palace

When Marcia's friend gave her two tickets to visit the State Rooms and Royal Mews she asked if I might like to join her, as one of my fifty things. It wasn't an entry on my original Bucket List but as I've never actually been inside Buckingham Palace, it was a great one to include. I'd been lucky enough to have met the Queen, over twenty-five years ago, at the presentation of new Colours to HMS Dolphin. Steve was one of a small group chosen to be introduced to her, with their spouses, for an informal chat after the ceremony. A great honour. I appreciate that she is well briefed before such events but hearing her speak to each person in turn, I was fascinated by the way she talked to all of us individually. The questions she asked were informed and relevant, listening to our responses with interest, displaying the ability to put even the most nervous person at ease within moments. It's hard to imagine doing that day after day with such enthusiasm, be it real or perceived. Surely, it's hard not to be impressed by her professionalism, whatever your thoughts might be about the Royal Family. I wonder just how many people she has had to make polite conversation with over the years and how many discussions she actually remembers? Not that I was expecting her to remember me … or even be at home on the day we went to Buck House (although if she was, it would be nice to pop my head around the door to say "hello" again).

Marcia and I met up at Green Park and made our way to the Palace, just in time to see the Changing of the Guard, before our self-guided morning tour. We were issued audio guides, which steered us through the amazing rooms. We got a real feel for the history, enjoyed the art collection and marvelled at the mechanics and organisation of this working palace. Though I think it would be fair to say Marcia struggled a little with the technology. Despite being "Mrs" KC The Gadget Man, I actually consider myself a bit of a technophobe. However, compared to my sister that day, I have to say I was a bit of a genius, able to select the correct sequence of buttons to get her back on track when her audio guide was out of sync and even getting her rebooted at one point. Not that it was complicated, it's just not her thing, but then nothing that remotely resembles a gadget (including remote controls) really is, which is why Mr C likes to tease her mercilessly about it!

We strolled at a leisurely pace through each of the State Rooms, immersing ourselves in the splendour of it all. The end of the tour leads you out into the grounds, with the Garden Café situated on the Palace's West Terrace. It was such a beautifully warm day, we treated ourselves to tea and cake in the sunshine, looking out across the splendid lawns. It was so tranquil it seemed almost impossible that we were actually in the centre of our busy, cosmopolitan, capital city. Suitably refreshed, we followed the meandering path around the gardens, towards the exit, ready for our afternoon visit to the Royal Mews. State vehicles, both horse-drawn and motorised, are housed here, including the Gold State Coach which has been used for Coronations for nearly two hundred years. Then our afternoon finished with a visit to the stables, where the Windsor Grey and Cleveland Bay horses (used to pull the royal carriages) are kept and trained. It was a delightful day out and a real pleasure to be a tourist in my own country. Thanks Marcia.

Chapter Twenty-Five
(11th - 15th September 2015)
Go Clubbing in Ibiza

We've been to Ibiza a couple of times. The first was a family holiday with Josh when we stayed at Puerto San Miguel, in the north of the island. It was October and things were closing down for the end of the season and I mean <u>literally</u> closing down. On our last day, before checking out, we asked our hotel if it would be possible to keep our room for the rest of the day, as we had a late evening flight. We were told, very casually, that this would not be a problem as there would be nobody there. So, if we could just turn the lights out and drop the key behind the desk on our way out that would be great!

Our second visit was with Craig and Caroline. This time we stayed in the south, at the very beginning of the season in April. We'd managed to pick up a ridiculously cheap and cheerful deal, flying with a budget airline from Bournemouth Airport, staying at an all-inclusive hotel in San Antonio. Our rooms were on the top floor, serviced by a lift that operated something like Arkwright's till in Open All Hours. You took your life in your hands getting in and out of that thing. There was no pattern to when the doors would open and close, their timing was completely random and the speed with which they shut was ferocious. It was like playing Russian roulette! The food was poor and the beverages were served in the flimsiest of plastic cups, with a limit of two drinks per person for each trip to the bar. However, the clientele was "interesting" ... which meant the people watching was fascinating.

There was absolutely no atmosphere in the main bar, which was lit by dazzlingly bright fluorescent strip lights, so to make up for the lack of ambience we devised a way to keep ourselves entertained. We would put our four chairs in a row, backs to the wall, enabling us to sit and watch all the comings and goings of our fellow holidaymakers without missing a thing. It was great. We picked up quite a few fashion tips. For the ladies; any combination of animal prints, the tighter the better and for the gents; football shirts or wife-beater vests, teamed with either very short or knee length sports shorts (nothing in-between) and trainers (which would never see the inside of a gym) or sliders. Another great game was to work out exactly who was with whom, by watching the social interaction between the aforementioned ladies and gentlemen, which seemed to change not just day-by-day but hour-by-hour... and that was amongst the middle-aged generation! There was only so much of this heady excitement we could take in on one night, so after a while we would head out onto the "Strip". As it was so early in the season, not everywhere was open yet but of the places that were, The Buccaneero Bar became our favourite late night hang out. We knew it was another classy joint when, on the first night, we ordered a gin and tonic and were asked if we wanted a pint or a half! At only five Euros it made financial sense to request a pint. It was good fun there because the people were generally a little younger and the music was great. Whenever *Moves Like Jagger* was played, the bar staff would stop whatever they were doing and perform their own, well-choreographed routine behind the bar. We had such a laugh on that holiday that Caroline decided we should make a return trip … only this time we needed to go Clubbing!

Now come on, Clubbing in Ibiza has GOT to be one for the List. This time we decided to go in September, once the family holidays were over, so it wasn't swarming with kids. We started looking at the end of September, phoning a couple of companies for quotes but the prices were extortionate. During one call, a very helpful young man started questioning our requirements in more detail, trying to help us find something suitable. We explained that we were primarily heading to Ibiza to go Clubbing. "So, are you specifically targeting the Closing Parties?" he asked. "Err … no" was our reply, trying to sound like seasoned clubbers who knew what we were talking about. "Then may I suggest mid-September, before those parties start, as that's what makes the end of September so expensive" and when he did those costings, the price came down considerably. We also explained that we wanted to stay in an all-inclusive hotel in San Antonio. "Are you sure" he asked "it's just … you don't really sound like a San Antonio kind of lady" … bless him! I told him about our previous stay in San Antonio and the fact that we knew exactly what we were letting ourselves in for. Actually, when we told him the name of the hotel we'd stayed in previously he said, "Oh yes, you do know what you're letting yourself in for but I think I can get you something a bit better than that for your money" and he did.

This year's hotel was much nicer. In fact, playing in the pool one day, Caroline said something along the lines of "I'm really impressed with this hotel, it's like being on a proper holiday". Our only slight issue was that, due to family commitments, we could only manage a long weekend and this limited us a little on our Clubbing options. I quite fancied a Flower Power or Vintage themed night (obviously) but unfortunately, they weren't running on the days we were there. As luck would have it, Mr C was discussing our plans with one of his clients, who just so happened to have connections at Pacha and offered to get us put on the guest list for the Friday night. How exciting! The problem was, we were arriving on a very early flight from Gatwick Friday morning ... so early in fact, that we didn't bother going to bed the night before and Pacha didn't actually open until midnight. Avoiding the temptation to take a nap (pre-clubbing) we powered on through, running more on adrenalin (well, the girls at least) than energy. By the time we finally got there, we'd been up for over forty hours. That didn't stop Caroline and I having a good old boogie but it did stop us staying until it closed. Although, despite our weariness, we still managed to pop into our old haunt, The Buccaneero Bar, for a quick nightcap (around 4am) on the way home.

We slept well that night/morning. Well ... but not for very long. You see, with our restricted timescale, we were on a bit of a mission. Caroline really wanted to go to the Hippy Market at Santa Eulalia but Saturday was our only opportunity and it was only open from 10am until 2pm. At least, I'm SURE that's what I read on the leaflet when I insisted everyone set their alarms to get up in time to make the visit worthwhile. However, when we got there, we discovered it was actually open from 10am ... until 10pm! Oh well, at least we had extra time to have a good wander around ... and we weren't wasting that lovely sunshine by sleeping the day away. Sunday was, of course, a day of rest. We needed it after the hectic preceding days. We spent the whole day sunbathing by the pool, popping in for a quick dip to cool off now and then ... and snoozing. Fully refreshed, that night we were back at The Buccaneero Bar, working our way through the cocktail menu - well, part of it (it was a very long menu). As we'd hired a car for the weekend (which ironically worked out cheaper than booking four return airport transfers) we spent Monday on the beach at Cala Tarida, sunbathing, swimming, playing in the surf and having lunch on the beach. A relaxing end to a frenetic weekend and a bit of a recharge before returning to our busy lives the following day, when we were going to be hot and heavy into the final preparations for getting Josh off to Uni ... or so we thought!

When Josh did his UCAS application, he was adamant he wanted to go to the University of Westminster and listed list different courses rather than different Universities when he had to make his choices in order of preference. Knowing this was going to be a full-on year for all of us I'd planned ahead, making a note of the dates for Freshers' Week and the start of semester from the University's website. Working with this information, I had set aside the weekend of September 19th to move him into Halls. When, in August, he got his formal offer of a place, it was all systems go to formalise his accommodation in Raffles House. However, when the contract came through it said that he was able to move in from September 12th. Much to his disappointment, moving in this early wouldn't be possible. Our Ibiza trip had been booked way back in February and we wouldn't be home until Tuesday 15th, with work commitments filling the rest of that week. He was not impressed but there was nothing I could do.

When we landed at Gatwick on the Tuesday morning, I turned my phone on so that the taxi driver meeting us could make contact. Sure enough, a text message immediately pinged through. That's prompt, I thought … until I saw who the text was from and what it said;

Hi Mum. Just to let you know I am up at Raffles House with Mark at the moment. Charlie and Jos have come with us to see what it's like as well. We will be heading back Wednesday morning so that I am home for Grandma's birthday dinner. We have taken a couple of bags with us which are mainly bed sheets etc! Hope you had a great time in Ibiza and I'll see you Wednesday! Xxx

I love the fact that I have such a confident, independent son but REALLY?!? Talk about being deprived of that special, tear-soaked moment when parents deliver their precious offspring to their new life in the adult world. Thanks Josh, unconventional as always.

Chapter Twenty-Six

(25th September 2015)

Ride the longest zip line in Europe

I believe I have some of the most thoughtful, generous friends anyone could wish for and I received some amazing gifts for my birthday this year, more than one of which was a perfect entry for the List ... like this one. As I've said before, I am not particularly sporty and despite my previous exploits, I'm not an out-and-out adrenaline junkie. I prefer to think of myself as a "let's give it a go" kind of girl who doesn't like missing out on an opportunity. So generally, if someone says, "Would you like to ... xyz", as long as it's not TOO far outside my comfort zone, I generally say "yes".

A few years ago, Mr C and I had read about Zip World in North Wales and its plans to open the longest zip line in Europe. We agreed that it was something we'd both like to do at some point. Little did we know it was going to be now.

When Maggie, John, Linda and Jim arrived with our Tour T-shirts the night before we went to Morocco, we were thrilled when they also presented us with a voucher to go zipping for my birthday, adding that they would come with us. Trying to find a date that we could all do wasn't easy though. We didn't want to go during peak holiday season and trying to find a weekend that all six of us could make proved to be impossible. Linda and Jim were in the process of moving to a new house, meaning they couldn't commit to anything too far in advance, whereas we needed to plan ahead as our diary this year was already ridiculously full. Sadly, we had to admit defeat and ended up booking as just a foursome with Maggie and John for this exhilarating experience.

Before I talk about zipping, I need to go off piste again, to talk a little about the home that Linda and Jim were about to move out of. The Madhouse was a house that held many fond memories. They'd lived there for as long as I'd known them (since Josh and Jamie were toddlers) and it's just a stone's throw from our house. It's a home which has hosted many a social gathering over the years, but without doubt, the funniest has to be the very first Burns Night we celebrated together, which I hinted at earlier. It was one of those fantastic nights that started well, then just got better and better, turning into one of the most hysterical nights of our lives. We were a group of eight that night, Linda and Jim (of course), Maggie and John, Sharon and TC and us. We each played a part; addresses, toasts, responses, recitals and entertainment, interpreting our roles in our own unique ways to create an informal Burns Night based, very loosely, on the traditional format. When we could eat and drink no more, we pushed the table and chairs to one side and danced into the wee small hours, until we could dance no more. Even poor Linda and Jim, who NEVER go to bed before tidying up after entertaining, just closed the dining room door and retired that night/morning. Coming down to face the devastation when they surfaced, it soon became obvious that a bit more than clearing up was required. In fact, they ended up having to redecorate but both agreed it was so worth it. I am not exaggerating when I say our faces and ribs were ached the following day because we had laughed so much the night before.

That wasn't the only Burns Night we celebrated at The Madhouse. The next one was even bigger, both in numbers of participants and the space we needed. After the formalities (read informalities), we moved from the dining room into the conservatory for some proper Scottish Country Dancing and a game of Pin the Sporran on Sean Connery (a life-sized cut out, not the man himself)! Then it was out into the garden, which was very frosty that particular January night, for our very own Highland Games, which included that family favourite Fling the Welly. With each toss, TC would shout "Mark that, Sharon" and Sharon would dutifully gallop off into the darkness to find the flung wellie, marking it by sticking her umbrella in the ground (not that we could see it in the pitch black) to determine the winner.

Another favourite Madhouse tradition that evolved over the years was Christmas Eve. The real start of Christmas for me is the Christmas Eve Carol Service at St Peters Church in Titchfield village, which culminates in a candlelit procession around the church, singing carols, continuing out into the street to wish everyone a Merry Christmas and the annual competition to see who can get the furthest without their candle going out on the walk home. Now, because The Madhouse is strategically placed between the church and our house, it is en-route either to or from the service. It started one year with us just "popping in for a quick one", which then became an expectation for every subsequent Christmas Eve. Jim's Dad used to make wicked Brandy Alexanders, which we soon discovered were best consumed after the service. If consumed before, it would render you unable to regulate your singing volume and somehow encourage you to compete with the choir when aiming for those high notes … which I don't think our fellow parishioners particularly appreciated. So, the ritual began that we'd bimble down to the church, exercise our vocal cords with a few carols then stop to lubricate them on the way home. Jim's Dad would keep the Brandy Alexanders flowing, whilst simultaneously talking man-to-man and putting the world to rights with a young Josh, which is generally what under tens do on Christmas Eve isn't it??? When we lost Jim's Dad it seemed disrespectful to break the tradition, so Jim took the helm. It took him a while to get his recipe just right but being the good friends (and chief tasters) we are, we soldiered through with him until he perfected his formula. We do seem to get through an obscene amount of cream and brandy … but it is Christmas.

One year, Linda and Jim decided not to come to church, as they were entertaining that night and had too much preparation to do. With their guests arriving later that evening, we decided to defy convention and call in before the service, to give them time to get ready. A Brandy Alexander or two later, we realised we really needed to get a wiggle on if we wanted to get to the church on time. We bid them farewell and set off at a trot, albeit a bit of a wobbly trot. About a hundred yards down the road, we looked at our watches and realised we were never going to make it in time, so turned around and headed straight back to The Madhouse. We'd returned so quickly that they hadn't even had time to rinse our glasses … so it seemed the obvious thing to do was refill them and keep Linda and Jim company until their guests arrived. What thoughtful friends we are. As I said before, they've sold The Madhouse now, so we'll just have to start creating more memories in their new home, although perhaps minus the redecorating!

Back to Zip World. We drove up to Betws y Coed on the Thursday night. We'd decided to make it a long weekend, in case the weather turned against us. That way, if Friday was no good, at least we had Saturday and at a push Sunday, to reschedule. Emma and Nathan told us how they had driven up, all the way from Wiltshire, to ride Velocity. Just as they arrived, the wind picked up and it was so strong the zip line had to be closed. They had to go home and return to North Wales two weeks later for a second attempt - which proved successful but had been a bit of a pain. Hence, we were hedging our bets. Luckily for us the forecast for the following day was good.

After checking-in at our accommodation, we headed down to the Royal Oak for liquid refreshment after our long journey. It was a lovely evening, so we sat outside in the pretty Beer Garden. My diary entry for that night reads *"Beer and fairy lights ... what could be better?"*. The next morning the weather was perfect, so we set off for Blaenau Ffestiniog to take on Titan, the first four-person zip line in Europe, which the website describes as;

The ultimate group zipping experience and currently the largest zip zone in Europe. Zipping in a seated position, you are afforded stunning views over Blaenau Ffestiniog and down the valley ahead. Zip World Titan encompasses three zip lines. Each rider travels over two thousand metres. The total length of the zip lines is over eight thousand metres!

Oh yes, we were up for some of that. We were kitted out with helmets, goggles and very attractive red flying suits. Maggie has a great photo of John and I walking across the car park, which my diary refers to as our "Top Gun Moment - dressed to thrill!".

Ready for action, we were driven up to the start of the first zip line, Alpha, which is the longest of the three. There were about twenty of us in total and you take it in turns to ride, four abreast, which was great for us as it meant we could all ride together. You make your way up onto, what could best be described as, a metal cattle grid with a sliding gate in front of you, similar to the starting gates at horse races. You are clipped onto the zip line, then you get seated in your harness and put your feet up on the bar below the gate. When you have all been checked and double checked, the gates slide open simultaneously and you're off! You are so high that, to begin with, you don't realise you're travelling at seventy miles an hour but when you look down and see your shadow racing across the ground below it puts it all in perspective.

The end of the zip line is ... interesting. You approach it at such speed that, although you know the arresting wires will slow you down in time, your brain tries to tell you otherwise. Although, being very light, Maggie would stop so abruptly that her legs would swing up in the air, almost touching the zip line above her. For the rest of us that wasn't an issue! Once everyone is down, it's a short walk to Bravo zip line for a repeat performance and then on to the last zip line, Charlie, which takes you back to the slate cavern where you started, flying high over the buildings as you come in to land. It was a brilliant experience and if I had to sum it up in one phrase it would be "We came, we saw, we conquered and we all had an absolute blast". Thanks for a great present my great friends.

Chapter Twenty-Seven

(2nd October 2015)

Go on a Kayak Safari in Cornwall

I believe I may have mentioned, more than once, that we love both Ruby or campervan and kayaking. We also love our annual trips to Cornwall towards the end of the summer, when the West Country is much quieter, so you can imagine just how much we love combining all three. This year was no exception, especially with it being "my" year, so the date had been in the diary for some time. On these occasions, we are creatures of habit and use the same campsite, partly because we only go for a short break so it's good to have our bearings from the get-go and partly because it's a great location for all the things we want to do. We stay at Mother Ivey's Bay Holiday Park at Trevose Head because a) it has great views b) it has two very different beaches within walking distance, one being a private beach on site and c) we're close to our beloved Padstow, where that sweet local nectar that is Doom Bar Real Ale doesn't have to travel too far (yes I know … but don't start being a purist, talking about the location of Doom Bar breweries and bottling plants … let me live in my little bubble, it's a happy place).

So, the date was set and Ruby was prepped, packed and ready for departure, except this year we seemed to have an extra passenger. Reg, our faithfully moggy, was having separation issues with Josh now away at University. He would prowl, or should I say howl, around the house looking for him. With Josh being a teenage night owl, Reg was used to him coming home in the early hours and now took to sleeping in his room at night, presumably just in case he did come home. During the day, this pining pussycat was my shadow, following me around and getting under my feet, constantly demanding attention. It got so pathetic that I tried getting Josh to FaceTime him but that didn't really help, in fact if anything it made him worse. Imagine his distress when he saw me packing up the van. He knew the signs and he knew what it meant. He may not be the brightest crayon in the box but he knew abandonment when he saw it. I only had to get a suitcase out of the loft and the second I opened it to pack he'd be sitting inside it, defying me not to complete my task because he knew that meant we'd be away for a while.

On this occasion, packing the van was no exception. In a final act of rebellion, as I reached up to close the tailgate, he moved quicker than I've ever seen him move before, launching himself into the van, staring at me as if daring me to try to evict him. I offered calming words and affection, gently lifting him from his perch but he was having none of it. Claws firmly clenching the crocheted blanket (sadly not the one I'd intended to make when Ruby was conceived in France – but I'll come to that a bit later) he was determined he wasn't going anywhere. As we weren't actually setting off until the next day, I decided to leave him to it, leaving the tailgate open for him to keep his dignity and retreat of his own accord. Finally, hunger got the better of him and several hours later he stood down from his post to grab a quick Scooby Snack from the kitchen. Seizing my moment, although with pangs of guilt, I rushed out and shut the door. With a look of contempt, he slunk away, retreating to Josh's bed in the hope of some solace there.

The following day he refused to make eye contact as we said goodbye. I think we must pander to that cat far too much! We set off after the evening rush hour, arriving at our destination just before midnight. The end of September is shoulder season and the chances of our pitch not being available from first thing the following morning were pretty slim. We parked up for the night in the lay-by that the surfers use, just outside the campsite gate, so we'd be ready to rock nice and early. The beauty of our van is that we take our bed with us, so why pay for an extra night in the campsite if we'd only get to use it for a few hours. We awoke to blue skies and sunshine and after breakfast I bimbled into the campsite office, using the pathetic excuse that we had "driven through the night to avoid traffic" asking if it would be possible to get onto our pitch early. Luckily for us the pitch was vacant (no real surprise there) so we were able to go straight in. By 10am we were installed in our prime spot with sea views, ready for adventure!

Usually Craig and Caroline join us for our annual trip but this year they were unable to, which meant we were travelling light. Not travelling light because our besties weren't with us but travelling light because it was just us (minus cat), so instead of towing Daisy (see Chapter 12 if you've forgotten who she is) who is usually fully loaded with an awning, a fire pit, surfing stuff, kayaking gear (including Craig and Caroline's) with TWO huge Ocean Kayaks strapped on top, this year it was just us, our boogie boards and our inflatable kayak ... all in the van, with no trailer ... ergo travelling light.

Now, the first thing I have to do once we've made camp, without exception, is walk down to the private beach and get my feet in the sea. Once I do that, I KNOW I've arrived. This year was no different, except it was completely different. Every other year the waves have been pounding our little bay but this year the sea was calm and I mean flat calm. It was like it was meant to be because normally we'd have the Ocean Kayak, designed to withstand substantial swell and perfect for catching a wave to surf in on. This year we were in the inflatable, which is pretty robust but not great for the high seas. Excited by the opportunity that presented itself we rushed back to the van to get our kit, grabbed a couple of pasties and cans of coke for an impromptu picnic and set off.

We've previously paddled from Polventon Bay, around Trevose Head to Constantine Bay and had always wanted to explore further along the coast, so this time decided to put in at Treyarnon Bay to see how far west we could get. As is our way, we didn't think about researching whether the sea conditions were likely to change, we just took the bull by the horns, drove to Treyarnon Bay, parked up, pumped up and set sail. The conditions were perfect for a kayak safari, paddling in and out of the caves and coves. I always find seeing the coastline from the sea a remarkable experience. The topography and strata are awesome along the Cornish coast, as is the birdlife. Cormorants dived around us, staying submerged for what seemed like forever, leaving us guessing where they would pop up. Oystercatchers skimmed the surface of the water and in one cove we were lucky enough to watch a Kingfisher fishing. It was all very special. We paddled as far as Bedruthan Steps, one of our favourite stretches of Cornish coastline that we've explored many times on foot. The tide was out and the sand exposed, so we thought that would be a great place to stop for our picnic. Paddling close to shore, we saw a man kneeling down to frame a shot of us through a natural stone arch. Busy posing for the anonymous gentleman, we didn't actually notice the sandbar we were approaching. We prepared to step out of the kayak and at the very moment a gentle ripple caught us side on, bringing us to an abrupt halt on the unseen obstacle and causing us to make a very undignified exit.

Slightly damper than we'd hoped, we hauled the kayak onto the beach. Grateful of the opportunity to stretch our legs, we thought we'd do a spot of rock-pooling before lunch and whilst doing so, recognised the photographer, still taking pictures. Rather presumptuously we introduced ourselves and asked if he'd captured our arrival (pre-capsize). We were delighted when he said he thought he had. Never one to be backward in coming forward, I asked if there was any chance that he could forward us a copy. Quick as a flash his wife stepped forward to get our email address and true to his word, in due course, he obliged. Admittedly you'd have to know it was us, silhouetted on the sea but we know and are delighted to have such a fab photograph with such a great story behind it.

Refreshed from our late lunch, we decided to put our sensible heads on and paddle back (rather than onward to the point of exhaustion resulting in the journey home being a ridiculously long slog, often against the tide ... which is what we would usually do). We'd achieved all that we'd hoped for and more ... and this was only day one of our Cornish adventure.

Chapters Twenty-Eight & Twenty-Nine

(3rd October 2015)

Cycle the Camel Trail

&

Ride a tandem

Every time we've visited Padstow, we've always said "One of these days we really should cycle the Camel Trail", a bridleway over seventeen miles long, which follows the path of two former railway lines from Padstow to Wenford Bridge, via Wadebridge and Bodmin. We'd never done it, partly because we'd never actually figured out how to get our bikes onto Daisy as, with everything else piled inside and on top of her, there was nowhere to attach a cycle carrier. Having put it off for far too long, we thought that, by putting the Camel Trail on the Bucket List, we'd have to find a way to make it happen. As we weren't taking the trailer this year it would be possible to put the bike rack on Ruby's tow bar. The trouble was, we knew we'd be arriving late for our wild camping in the lay-by on the first night, needing access to the back of the van to make up the bed. We could, of course, easily take the bikes off to do this, then put them back on to secure them for the night (you can't exactly lock your bikes to a hedgerow) but this seemed a bit of a faff, particularly as we'd only actually be using them for the one day. The obvious answer was to hire bikes when we got there, which is actually what most people doing this ride do. Problem solved! Impressed with our forward planning, I took it one step further and bought myself a pair of cycle shorts, in preparation, from a leading discount supermarket. Having invested £4.99 I felt committed! We knew the campsite would have information on hire centres, so we were sorted. The morning we'd checked in to Mother Ivey's Bay, I'd gathered an assortment of leaflets about the companies offering rental and the types of bikes that were available. Imagine my delight when I saw that hiring a tandem was an option. I was going to be able to do tick two things off my List on the same day!

I've enjoyed my cycling over the years, despite being a late learner. In fact, my Dad always used to say "That child will never learn to ride a bike" as, having removed my stabilisers, he would spend hours holding on to the back of me as I wobbled around the garden, falling over as soon as he let go. I did get there, eventually, although I have never been a confident rider. Steve and I purchased state of the art Muirhead Marin Mountain Bikes in the 1980s, as it was the trendy thing to do but I soon discovered that off-roading was never really my thing. I'm still a bit precarious perched on top of two wheels. I go downhill slower than I go uphill and still get confused about which gear does what. However, not one to let mere details get in the way, Mr C and I have done a little bit of gentle cycling over the years. In fact, our very first date was a day out cycling in the New Forest. He should have seen the signs then but perhaps he mistook my squeals of fear for shrieks of delight. He's persevered with me though and we've have had some interesting cycling adventures ... with mixed success.

We did want to cycle some of the canal towpaths, initially putting that as an entry on my Bucket List. I even got as far as researching a three-day trip, from Bath to Reading but when I spoke to the chap in the ticket office at the train station, he said we couldn't reserve bike spaces on trains, as they are strictly limited, so would have to take pot luck on the day! Not very helpful when a fundamental part of the plan is being able to get your bike to the starting point and also being able to get it home again. Then, when I tried to book accommodation for the dates we'd set aside, I discovered it coincided with a Cheese Festival en-route, meaning all the local accommodation was fully booked (I didn't realise Cheese Festivals were such a big thing). So, I took these as omens and we shelved the idea. Maybe one day I'll revive my plans ... perhaps for my 60th Birthday Bucket List!

Another time we thought it would be "fun" to cycle around the Isle of Wight. Living on the South Coast, we look at the Isle of Wight all the time. In fact, when we initially bought our Ocean Kayak, we had grand plans to paddle across the Solent to the island as it's only about a mile-and-a-half away (as the crow flies). We mentioned this to the water sports guy who'd sold us our vessel, who said "Great idea. I guess you've got your two-way radios and support vessel to get you across the shipping lanes sorted?". OK, so not one of our better ideas after all.

Circumnavigating the island on a bike seemed a much more realistic challenge. We picked a weekend when the weather was due to be perfect. It was only sixty-five miles around the island and although we hadn't done any training for it, what could possibly go wrong? Well, to start with MY interpretation was that we would drive to Gosport, unload our bikes, take the ferry from Gosport to Portsmouth, the ferry from Portsmouth to Ryde and THEN start cycling. However, Mr C decided the nine-mile ride from home to the Gosport Ferry would be a good warm up and save us the parking fees, so we set our alarm for silly o'clock on the chosen day and sallied forth. The weather was glorious and the initial cycle certainly warmed us up. I can't remember the exact timings now but when we reached Ryde, we were certainly ready for breakfast.

Fuelled up, we set off in a clockwise direction, estimating it would take about eight hours, factoring in lunch. Pretty much as soon as we left Ryde it became apparent that eight hours would be "optimistic". Until you actually pay attention, I don't think you realise just how hilly the whole island is. Bearing in mind that, as I said, I go slower downhill than up, it was looking unlikely that we would manage a complete circuit in less than a week! Not wanting to put ourselves under additional pressure, we decided to just keep going and see how far we could get. We didn't get very far. By Shanklin I had to stop at a corner shop to get some ibuprofen because my knees were killing me. We decided to take an early lunch break there, to let the painkillers kick in. I wasn't totally sold on the results of my medication but we pushed on to Ventnor, hoping that getting on the move again would ease my aching limbs. It didn't, so at the bottom of the very big hill that you have to descend to get to Ventnor we decided to call it a day and head back ... back up the very big hill we'd just come down!

By the time we'd got back to Sandown I was done ... so we jumped on a train and bought a ticket to Ryde - quite literally. We'd only managed about a quarter of the island and I was feeling a bit of a failure, sore and very sorry for myself. As a consolation, Mr C said he would treat me to a doner kebab for tea when we got back to Gosport (he spoils me that boy). I was ridiculously excited. I hadn't had a kebab since my student days in Bournemouth, when it was the food of choice after the nightclubs had kicked out ... which in those days was about 1am! Wearily I pushed my bike onto the ferry back to Portsmouth, then the ferry back to Gosport, perking up a bit for the short walk to the kebab house. Luckily for us they had seating, so I collapsed in a heap at the table while Mr C purchased heaven in a polystyrene box. By the time it arrived I could hardly eat it, I was so tired. "Eat half and take half home for supper" he suggested. A brilliant idea ... except ... I'd forgotten ... home was a nine-mile cycle away. We didn't talk much on the journey home. With my "treasure" in a plastic carrier bag, dangling from my handlebars, I was head down and teeth clenched, unable to say a word. So, as I say, mixed results with bikes to date. Hopefully this time was going to be different.

The morning after our kayak safari, I called the cycle rental office to see if they had a tandem available. They asked our heights and said they had one which should be ideal, so we reserved it. By mid-morning we were in Wadebridge, getting measured up for our trusty steed. Saddles adjusted, the young man told us to ride a few yards down the path, to check it was OK. There was some debate about who should go at the front. Obviously, I thought it should be me, as I would then be in charge of the one and only set of brakes (naively I thought there'd be two), which I use frequently when I'm cycling. Mr C said it should be him because if I had control of our speed, we'd never make it. Also, he was far more competent with the gears than me (true). Sensing a marital disagreement, the young man tactfully suggested it was normally the taller person at the front, so I was forced to concede. Technicalities sorted, we climbed aboard and quick as a flash we were off ... then quick as a second flash we weren't, which was probably due to my hysterical screaming, use of a few choice words and struggling to stop myself bursting into tears. I didn't like it! My balance was all over the place and I was totally out of control. I dismounted as quickly as I could and said, "Take it back, we'll take two single bikes".

Still within earshot of the young man (about ten yards), Mr C calmly suggested that I try it for a little bit longer before making my decision. He said we'd take it really slowly until I got my confidence. Quivering like a jelly, I eventually agreed to give it another go. I thought that if I just focused on Mr C's back and tried to relax, I could calm myself down. It appeared to work and I was soon feeling much better about the whole thing ... until he said "OK, we need to turn around now". It took more shrieking and pleading, followed by a rapid dismount by me, before he was able to do the U-turn back to the shop. "We'll take it" said Mr C, quite clearly much to the young man's surprise, "where do we pick up the trail?". I was beginning to regain my composure, helped by the fact that we were going to be on a relatively flat bridle path, with no motorised traffic. Telling myself to get a grip, I climbed back on and even managed a smile. "OK" the young man said, "so you go up the road here, over the first roundabout, over the second roundabout then it's on your left, you can't miss it". "Hang on a minute!" I exclaimed, my panic rising again "What's all this talk about roads and roundabouts? I thought the Camel Trail was a bridleway?". "Oh yes, it is … apart from this little bit through town before you get going" he chirpily replied. "We'll be fine" said Mr C "I'll take it nice and slow, like we did just now". With a slightly weaker smile and a nervous laugh I agreed to give it a go, with the proviso that, if I said stop at any time, he had to stop.

Ground rules in place, we were finally off. There were an anxious few minutes as we started on relatively narrow roads, amongst busy Saturday traffic but with considerably less squeaks and whimpers than on our trial run, we were on our way. "Coming up to the first roundabout now" says Mr C. "Stop!" says me and he dutifully stopped. "I'm walking around the roundabout" I said and before he could say anything, I was off and standing beside him. I walked across the road, while he negotiated his way through traffic and around the first roundabout, pulling up beside the pavement for me to get back on. A short time later he said, "Coming up to the second roundabout now but it's a mini one so stay on and I'll take it really slowly". I did … and so did he. Shortly after that we saw the signs to the bridleway and turned off onto a smaller residential road, then through some bollards and onto the trail. Gradually I began to relax a bit more. It was a couple of miles before I could take my eyes off the centre of his back and actually start looking around, by which time we had managed to up-tempo to a much more acceptable speed, i.e. faster than walking. There were still occasions when I would yelp and have an attack of nerves, like if we hit a pothole, or had to pass between concrete posts but as long as Mr C warned me in advance, I learnt to deal with my anxieties.

Towards the top end, the trail forks and we decided to visit Bodmin first, for a spot of lunch. Revitalised, we retraced our steps to the bridleway junction, then continued all the way to the end of the line. We celebrated with a comfort break at the appropriately named Snail's Pace Café. Refreshed once again, we set off back towards Wadebridge and by now I was relaxed and chatty, pointing out things of interest that I'd missed on the way up (when all I could see was the back of Mr C's t-shirt). It was all going so well ... until a dog ran out in front of us, causing Mr C to do an emergency stop. Panic stricken, my language was not very ladylike, cursing at the woman who had let her excitable dog run into our path. She was apologetic as she gathered him up ... together with her young children (who I hadn't noticed), presumably trying to distract them from this crazy lady giving her what for. Well, how was I to know there were children present? Sitting at the back, with self-imposed tunnel vision, I can only see what's going on once we've passed it. Picking up the pace, we left her well behind us. A little later, we stopped to take some photos and read an information board. I didn't think we'd been stationary that long and couldn't believe it when the family and their dog came striding by, glaring in my direction. We let them pass, hoping they might turn off somewhere, before setting off again. Sadly, it transpired that they'd remained on the bridleway and we were soon cycling past them again. Unbelievably, the dog ran out on us a second time and although Mr C didn't have to come to a complete stop, I couldn't help but vent my anger, rather loudly, about how people who couldn't control their dogs shouldn't let them off the lead. Luckily, we didn't see them again.

Returning to Wadebridge, I was quietly confident that I would be able to remain in the saddle as we cycled back through town to pick up the second part of the trail down to Padstow. Mr C was very good and kept me talking to take my mind off the cars passing close by. We were still chatting as we negotiated the roundabouts with ease and then the bridge. Hang on a minute, what bridge? "I don't remember crossing the river" said Mr C, "Neither do I" I replied. We'd been so busy nattering that we'd taken a wrong turn. "Don't worry" said Mr C "there's a roundabout at the end of the bridge, we'll turn around and go back". Now, although we'd had no issues on the other roundabouts (during the return journey), we were going to have to go all the way around this one … and it was a very small one. "I'm getting off" I said. "No, you're not" he replied and as he was the one with the brakes, I had no choice. I'm not sure who was more scared, me as we completed a full three-hundred-and-sixty-degree turn, screaming at the top of my voice, or the drivers in the cars waiting to join the roundabout from each of the side roads. We must have looked a right sight, however, mission accomplished we were soon back on track, quite literally.

The second part of the cycle from Wadebridge down to Padstow was picturesque as we followed the River Camel. We didn't really notice that it was a very gentle downhill gradient, pretty much all the way. It was a beautiful afternoon and our reward for reaching the other end of the trail was a portion of chips, which we enjoyed sitting on the harbour wall. The ride back to Wadebridge took a little longer than we expected because this time, we did notice the slight incline and by now we'd been on the go for quite a while. In total we'd cycled around forty miles which, including stops, took about seven hours. As we dismounted for the final time and parked our now beloved tandem back in the bike rack, I was a little saddle sore, despite my expensive cycling shorts but what hurt most were my hands … from hanging on so tight!

Chapter Thirty
(9th October 2015)

The "Pembrokeshire Surprise"

Each year we schedule a visit to spend a long weekend with our friends, Rob and Jo, who are renovating a lovely welsh cottage on the side of a mountain in a very beautiful part of Pembrokeshire. Some years the weather is grim, so we just light the fire, hunker down and spend the whole time eating, drinking and playing silly games. On such weekends, staying in our PJs the whole time is not unheard of. Some years the weather has been glorious and we've picnicked on the beach, been swimming in the sea (even in late October) and had some hilarious kayaking expeditions. In fact, it was Rob and Jo who first inspired us to get an Ocean Kayak. Rob LOVES his toys; guitars, surfboards, kayaks, skateboards, motorbikes ... some that he uses more than others. They'd purchased a two-man kayak shortly before one of our initial visits and showed it off with pride, even though they'd only used it once or twice.

As soon as we got home, we were doing our research and decided to buy one as a Family Christmas present that year ... Josh was thrilled! Who needs a new PlayStation when you can go kayaking with your Mum and Dad??? Anyway, we bought it and stored it, waiting for the weather to improve. During its maiden voyage on the Solent (which wasn't a crossing to the Isle of Wight), it seemed to be pulling to the left all the time. We wondered if it was something to do with the current, so took it for another outing up the River Hamble, where the same thing happened. We contacted the chap we'd bought it from (the one who'd listed the things we'd need if we were to cross to the Isle of Wight), who told us to bring it back down to his shop for him to have a look at. If there was nothing wrong with the kayak, he'd put us in the sea and watch us, to see where we were going wrong. Impressed with the great service, we took it down to show him and as soon as he turned it upside down, he noticed it had a twisted keel. It was obviously a manufacturing fault, so he replaced it with a new one straight away. Back in the water, we now found paddling in a straight line much easier and used it quite a lot.

We would take it to France when we went camping in the Vendee, where the Atlantic waves are perfect for surfing on and each year we would religiously take it to Pembrokeshire "just in case". Several times we did manage to go paddling with Rob and Jo. Once, when the sea was flat calm, we went coving around Newport and Dinas Head. Another time we paddled up the River Nevern, which is wide and calm to start with and then becomes narrow, shallow and quite fast flowing in places. We'd reached a part that looked like it could only be tackled one kayak at a time. If you've ever watched a line of cars trying to get up an icy hill, you'll know how everyone waits while the first car tries, giving it all they've got, either succeeding or sliding back down if they don't make it ... well, this stretch of the river looked a bit like that. We sat in the calm waters to the side, assessing the situation and decided that, if we gave it enough welly, we'd probably be able to get through the tricky bit. Leading the way, as the more experienced pair

(Rob and Jo only ever used their kayak when we visited!), we said, rather over-confidently, "Just watch us and do what we do". We paddled gently out into the fast running bit, then Mr C shouted "Go, go, go!" and we paddled as hard and fast as we could. Our arms may have been 'go, go, going' but the kayak certainly wasn't. We managed to move forward just a few feet but the river got very shallow, very quickly. By now our paddles were scraping on the stones beneath us and quite frankly, we just ran out of steam. As we stopped paddling the kayak turned slightly sideways and the rushing water, taking no prisoners, instantly capsized us. We stood up, laughing, just in time to see Rob and Jo giggling so hard at our ridiculous attempt that their uncontrollable chortling led to uncontrollable lack of stability ... and they fell off their kayak too! Clearly unable to navigate past this point, we accepted that we'd gone as far as we could and headed back down to the sea.

On another occasion we put in at Pwllgwaelod, with a plan to paddle to Fishguard Old Harbour, leaving a car at each end of the route so we only had to paddle one way. This time we'd checked which way the tide was running, to make sure we weren't paddling against it (we were learning). The weather was superb and the waves were gentle. We paddled at a leisurely pace, stopping off in a lovely little cove to have our picnic. When we set off again, the waves had picked up a bit and as we continued on, they picked up a bit more. Mr C and I were used to the waves in France but Rob and Jo weren't so keen and although Fishguard was in sight, sort of, they felt they needed to make another stop. Seeing a cove and with hardly any warning, they went for it ... so we felt obliged to follow. It was a very narrow cove, the entrance to which was between some quite big boulders and it was a bit hair raising surfing in. Luckily, we all landed without incident and hauled the kayaks out onto the stony beach. Poor Jo was visibly shaken by the experience and Rob had had enough. "That's it," he said, "we're not going any further". We all looked at the geography of the cove. The only way out was a steep climb up the cliff and there was no way we could carry the kayaks up there. Also, I'm not great at navigating steep cliffs at the best of times, so the thought of doing it carrying a kayak, wearing neoprene booties, swimwear and a life jacket did not appeal one little bit. I would far rather take my chances in the sea. "Don't worry about us" said Rob "we'll leave our kayak here and come back for it when the sea is calmer" but we knew that if he left it, he would never go back for it and it seemed such a shame to just abandon it. So, between us we hatched a plan. Rob and Jo would climb the cliff with their paddles and we would use the bungee cords, that we'd used to secure the picnic, to tie their kayak to the back of ours, enabling us to tow it back to Fishguard.

With their kayak attached, we prepared to get back in the water. We weren't exactly sure if it was possible to tow a kayak out into the surf, especially as the waves had increased in size while we'd been plotting. Mr C waded in as deep as he could, until both kayaks were in the water. I was already in the front of ours and he was holding us as steady as he could, waiting for a gap between the waves so he could jump on. The plan; as soon as he was aboard, I would paddle like mad, to stop us from being washed back to shore, until he was seated properly and ready to paddle too. Simple. The moment came and he made the leap of faith. Positions assumed, we just went for it, forging our way out through the swelling surf and past the break point. Once we'd negotiated the breakers, the paddle back to Fishguard wasn't too bad. We had to make some adjustments to our technique, to allow for the extra load but we were feeling quite chuffed with ourselves. We looked inland to see Rob and Jo waving their paddles. They were safely at the top of the cliff and had already reached the road. Rounding the corner into the Old Harbour, the water became much calmer, so we could relax and catch a gentle ripple to surf in on as our last little hoorah. We caught the perfect wave. Of course, what we hadn't accounted for was the fact that we still had the empty kayak tied to the back of us, which was considerably lighter than us and therefore much faster in the swell. As it came alongside us, we knew it was too late to try to untie it, so we just waited for the inevitable as it dragged us side-on to the waves and we tumbled out. A classy end to an adrenaline fuelled expedition.

Rob and Jo had known all about my List, as we'd discussed it during our visit the previous year. "Can you put an entry on it for me?" asked Jo, "Just call it Pembrokeshire Surprise". Her entry was duly included and I was relatively confident that it wasn't going to have anything to do with kayaking. The weekend of our annual trip arrived and we set off, after rush hour, on the Friday night, getting there just after midnight (our usual arrival time), to be greeted by good friends and a good bottle of wine. It wasn't going to be a late night, (in the past we've been known to be up chatting until 4am on the first night), as we had an early start for my surprise the next day. Not that we ever have really early starts in Pembrokeshire but it was going to be early for us!

Picnic packed (Rob is ALWAYS hungry and our days out ALWAYS include a picnic), we drove to Haverford West. I had no idea what was in store until we got to the Lifeboat Station and boarded a boat to Ramsey Island, which I'd heard about but never visited. Owned and managed by the RSPB, the island itself is less than two miles long, has an area of six-hundred-and-forty acres and its highest point is four-hundred-and-forty-six feet above sea level. As we docked on Ramsey Island, the first thing we saw was a three-day old Grey Seal pup on the beach just below us, calling for his Mum, who was swimming in the shallows. If you've ever heard a seal pup cry it sounds just like they are saying "Muuuum" in an almost human, childlike voice. So much so that, many a time, lifeboats have been called out when people have reported hearing a child trapped on a beach calling out for its Mum, only to find a seal pup there when they arrive. This little one was white and very scrawny but the Warden, who lives on the otherwise uninhabited island with his wife, explained how their growth rate was phenomenal, putting on over a pound in weight every day, so he'd soon be a chubby chap.

During his introduction, the warden's not the pup's of course, he told us there were various routes you could take to walk around the island. We set off clockwise, reaching a rocky pinnacle with fantastic views that was perfect for our picnic. After lunch, we continued to meander around the island. Each beach was littered with seal pups of various sizes, sunbathing, playing in the water or calling out to their Mums. They estimate four-hundred seal pups are born here each autumn. The noise was incredible. Away from the shore, we came across one of the herds of deer being led by a magnificent stag, some inquisitive rabbits and a wide variety of birds. It was amazing and so wonderful to be up close to nature in the raw.

Our return trip to the mainland was through the infamous Bitches, a stretch of water between Ramsey Island and the Welsh coastline, where the sea is squeezed over rocks on the seabed, changing the height of the water dramatically, causing the tide to flow at up to seven knots. It was a very exciting ride back. Just as we were about to dock on the mainland, our captain spotted a bull seal sitting in a tender. We went over to have a closer look, just as two of the lifeboat crew came to evict him because, apparently, this is something that happens quite often and they make a terrible mess. They tried pushing him with brooms but this just made him grumpy and he refused to budge. Bizarrely, he eventually jumped out and back into the sea when they threw buckets of water over him! It was hilarious. I'd managed to film their exploits and later, as requested, forwarded my footage to the ferry company, so they could pass it on to the lifeboat crew. Thanks Rob and Jo for my awesome birthday treat.

Chapter Thirty-One

(16th October 2015)

Visit Venice

Mr C also wanted to put a surprise entry on my List but I'd already stolen his idea of staying in a lighthouse, so he had to come up with something else. He decided upon a trip to Venice. He'd never been and the last time I was there was on a school trip, over thirty-five years ago, as part of an educational cruise on the SS Uganda (which subsequently got commandeered as a hospital ship during the Falklands conflict). I'd loved Venice and still have a charcoal drawing of the Rialto Bridge, which I'd bought from the artist while I was there. While doing our planning we took advice from Pam and Joe. Joe lived and worked in Venice for a number of years and they took regular trips back to visit. They recommended a lovely hotel, just off the beaten track, next to the train station, with easy access to everything. They also gave us some top tips of things to do and places to visit. It was going to be an action-packed long weekend.

Arriving in the afternoon, we checked into our hotel, then wandered into the centre to get our bearings and book tickets for The Show of Venice in the Teatro San Gallo, one of the recommendations from Pam and Joe. It's an entertaining, informative production, performed in English, giving an insight into the traditions and history of the city. We enjoyed it very much and found some of the things we learnt very useful over the next few days as we went exploring. The next morning the weather was bright and sunny, so we set off early, armed with our guidebook and the notes from Joe, ticking off most of the tourist highlights. We also wanted to see Venice from the water but rather than spending a fortune on a short trip in a Gondola, we decided to do something different.

Before we left, Pam had given me some leaflets and a newspaper which, knowing our trip was imminent, she had brought back from their recent visit. In the newspaper I noticed an advertisement for a kayak rental company, Venice By Water, offering guided tours. I emailed them to find out more, loved what they had to offer and made a booking. Their confirmation included the address of where we were to meet so, of course, we thought we knew where to go. However, one of the interesting things about Venice is that there are very few street signs. Even using Google Maps, although we knew we were in the right area, we just could not find the office. We phoned them to ask where they were and the directions they gave confirmed that we had, actually, previously been to the correct place, a courtyard with several closed doors … but no numbers. We told them we were on our way and when we re-entered the courtyard, one of the doors was now open and they were there to meet us. We filled in some paperwork and confirmed we'd like a two-man kayak. We'd assumed that we'd be on a tour with other people but as it happened, nobody else had booked. It turned out that they were a fairly new venture and they'd only just started advertising properly. It was a great set up though and I really hope they've managed to make a go of it.

Our guide asked what experience we had and we gave a brief outline (I didn't go into all the long stories you've had to suffer), which he was more than satisfied with. He said that lots of people said they had experience but when you put them in a kayak, they clearly didn't. He showed us to the changing room to get kitted out. Now, in the advert it said all equipment would be provided, so I must admit, I didn't think to take anything with us. I'd assumed (wrongly) we would be in an enclosed kayak, so we just wore jeans and t-shirts. However, when he showed us the kit to choose from it became clear that we were going to get wet! Not wanting to get our jeans soggy (travelling light, with only hand luggage, our clothing was minimal), we opted for stripping down to our underwear and t-shirts, covering our modesty with a pair of their sports shorts. At least that way we could go back to the hotel "commando" rather than traipsing from one end of Venice to the other in dripping denim. Climbing on the kayak from a doorway that opened directly onto the canal was … interesting but the water-level was quite high, so there was no big drop … you just had to step out horizontally. We sat down … and promptly got wet bottoms, so a good call on our choice of clothing!

Once we set off, our guide was happy that we knew what we were doing and said, "Just follow me". The turns are so tight that you can't see if anything is coming around the corner, so the non-powered craft have their own language to signal where they are and who has right of way. It was all very fascinating and a fantastic way to see the city. He took us to places that you could only get to by boat and showed us so many things that you wouldn't normally get to see as a tourist. Also, it's surprising just how many gardens there are in Venice. Take a look at Google Earth sometime, you'll be amazed. It was great to sample a taste of real Venetian life; the boat yards, floating markets, emergency services and utilities. It was something completely different and you certainly had to know what you were doing to navigate your way around as, at sea level and surrounded by buildings, none of the obvious landmarks were visible. Normally we've got quite a good sense of direction but here we lost our bearings very quickly. There's no way you could do it without a guide.

After winding through the quiet side canals for an hour or so, he said "OK, we're going to cross the Grand Canal now" and sure enough, just around the next corner, there it was. It looked very wide and VERY busy, with motorised craft whizzing up and down and water buses zig-zagging back and forth. "I want you to be ready to paddle as soon as I say go" he said. "Make sure you paddle fast and don't stop". Waiting on the edge of the canal, poised for action, it was hard to see when there would be a suitable gap for us to cross but he was an experienced chap and as soon as he gave the command, we were off. I've never experienced anything like that before and the description I gave people afterwards was that it was a bit like waiting to cross a motorway on a pushbike! His timing was perfect and we didn't feel in any danger but it certainly focuses the mind. In the end we were out for over two hours and thoroughly enjoyed every bit of it. Back at base, we packed our wet undies in a plastic bag and made our way back to the hotel, very pleased with our achievement.

That night, we decided to go for a meal in a restaurant close by, rather than fight our way back through the crowds to the centre. It was a lovely, traditional Italian meal and the food was great. By the time we'd finished it was close to closing and pretty much everyone had left, apart from one couple a few tables away from us. I'm not sure how we got chatting but we did and soon the maître d', assuring us that he was in no rush for us to leave, brought us a nightcap, on the house, to enjoy while they started clearing up around us. Tara and Fritz were a lovely couple from America, on a whistle-stop tour of Italy, followed by a cruise and were only in Venice for a couple of nights before heading off to Florence and Rome. We were getting on really well and the maître d' topped up our drinks. He again made it clear that he was happy for us to stay, so we moved over to our new friends' table and carried on chatting. It was a shame we'd met them at the end of the evening, rather than the beginning, as we really enjoyed their company but we felt guilty that we were stopping the restaurant from closing, so made our way to the bar to pay our bill. The maître d' gave us yet another drink. We were all paid up so, once our glasses were empty, we thanked him profusely and made our way out onto the pavement. We all still had so much to say to each other that we carried on with our conversation outside and were surprised when the maître d' appeared yet again with yet another drink! Fuelled by our many nightcaps, we talked about our plans to take the ferry over to Murano and Burano the following day. As it turned out, that's what Tara and Fritz hoped to do too. As we'd already researched tickets and timings, we said they were welcome to join us. They said they would like that very much and we arranged a meeting place and time, before finally saying goodnight and going our separate ways.

We wondered if it was the wine and liqueurs that had made them think spending the day with us was a good idea and didn't really expect to see them that morning. Arriving in good time, we waited for a bit but they didn't show. We were disappointed but not surprised. Just as we were about to go and get our tickets, they appeared! They'd overslept and were glad we'd waited. We had a really lovely time with them, watching the glass blowers in Murano and wandering around the pretty canals full of colourful houses in Burano. Tara and Fritz needed to be back in time for a pre-booked gondola trip, followed by a meal and we had tickets to a Vivaldi's Four Seasons concert at the Scuola Grande di San Teodoro, so we couldn't socialise into the evening. We exchanged details and said our final farewells, fully intending to keep in touch as we were hoping for a bit of a cheese-off (we were going to look into whether you can send cheese to and from America because we claim that Cheddar is the best but Fritz was adamant that Wisconsin produced the most fantastic cheese).

That evening, we found out where we needed to be for the concert, then looked for a restaurant close by for an early supper. It was a funny little eatery and somehow we ended up leaving by a different door than the one we'd come in through. Standing on the canal side, trying to get our bearings for the concert hall, we heard familiar voices and there, standing on one of the bridges, waiting for their gondola, were Tara and Fritz! What are the chances? If we hadn't gone the wrong way out of the restaurant, we wouldn't have bumped into them. We couldn't stop as our concert was about to start, so said farewell, yet again and left them to it.

Listening to the Four Seasons in such a magnificent concert hall, with the musicians in period costume, was like stepping back in time and very special. When it was over, we weren't ready to go back to the hotel, so instead decided to wander down to St Mark's Square to see it by night. We wound our way back through the narrow streets and alleyways, following the occasional sign (there aren't very many). We stopped on one corner, trying to work out which way to turn next, looking this way and that. Whilst faffing about, I glanced through the window of a restaurant and couldn't believe my eyes. Looking back at me were Tara and Fritz, having their meal! We waved but didn't go in. That would look a bit too much like we were stalking them, which we truly weren't. These had honestly been a series of chance encounters ... yet again! As it happens, that wasn't the last contact we had with them that night. We texted each other a few times, as they'd never been on a train before and were enquiring about the protocol of rail travel.

Sadly, we never did get to have our cheese-off. There are far too many rules and regulations about sending food across the pond and it seems you would need an export licence. We keep in touch though and one day, when we get to do our grand tour of America, we will definitely look them up.

Our last day in Venice was another full one, visiting the Basilica of Santa Maria Gloriosa dei Frari, going to the top of the San Marco Campanile in St Mark's Square for amazing views of the city, lighting a candle for Noel in St Mark's Basilica and finishing with a visit to the Doge's Palace and the Bridge of Sighs, before our evening flight home. It was an action packed few days in this truly iconic city. Thank you Mr C.

Chapter Thirty-Two
(24th October 2015)

Go to the Opera

It was certainly turning out to be a year of culture. I love live music and theatre and I've been to the ballet but never the opera. One of my early visits to Lanzarote was a diving holiday. I was due to be travelling alone, while Mr C went to visit his parents in Spain but Jim asked if I'd take Linda along with me as his surprise birthday treat for her. She wasn't a diver but other activities were available, so he signed her up for the surfing course. Not that she was a surfer either but she'd surfed a couple of times before, once in Lanzarote actually, as one of the activities I'd booked for us all on her fortieth birthday trip and also at Skern Lodge in Devon, so he thought she might like some lessons.

Although we shared accommodation, we did our own activities during the day, socialising together of an evening. I was in a group of half-a-dozen or so divers and buddied up with a crazy chick called Jane from London. We hit it off straight away and although we took our diving seriously, above the water we spent most of the time seeing the funny side of things. We became known to our dive leaders as the Dynamic Duo. Jane was travelling on her own, so we invited her to join us of an evening. We actually gathered quite an assorted social group in the end, individuals who'd booked with the same activity tour company, each doing a variety of things from diving and surfing to cycling and windsurfing. We had some fun nights out together after our active daytime programmes and as usual, all swapped details so we could to stay in touch. Jane and I corresponded almost as soon as we got home, sharing photos from our dives and following each other's antics on Facebook, as you do these days.

A year or so later, Mr C was due to visit his parents in Spain again and it was decided we would go together. I booked the flights then, shortly before we were due to leave, his mother decided I was no longer welcome. I wasn't entitled to a refund if I cancelled my flight, so decided to go anyway and look for something else to do. I found a dive centre and booked a hotel close by. As an afterthought, I decided to contact Jane to see if she fancied joining me. She works for the English National Opera, doing lighting and projection, so I knew her work schedule depended on the programme of productions and rehearsals but thought it was worth a shot. I sent her the details and was delighted when she said she was free and would love to come. She managed to find flights for the same days as mine, albeit from a different airport, I changed my booking for a single room to a twin, told the dive company there would now be two of us and the Dynamic Duo were reunited. It's an easy friendship, the sort that you can pick and put down without fear of recrimination. We had a fun few days (and nights), emailed a bit when we got back, then our communications tailed off again but I knew we wouldn't lose touch.

Fast forward to 2015. I told Jane all about my Bucket List. I told her I wanted to go to the Opera for the first time and asked her advice on what would be suitable for a beginner. She gave me a few suggestions. She also gave me dates of when things I might like would be on at the English National Opera, saying if I fancied any of them she may be able to get me tickets (as my Dad has always said, "It's not what you know but who you know"). I quite fancied the Barber of Seville and she came up trumps. She said she wouldn't be working on the night but that she'd leave the tickets at the box office and we could meet afterwards. I was very excited, both about the Opera and meeting up with my buddy again. I was even more excited when she said her friend Marc was working that night and if we arrived early, he would give us a backstage tour. I was very grateful and felt very privileged. We met Marc in the foyer. He handed us a programme, then gave us a full tour of the Colosseum, which is an incredible building. Up in the highest seats, at the back of the auditorium, he radioed somebody on stage, asking them to say something to demonstrate how amazing the acoustics are. He took us high up onto the gantries, to show us how they change the scenery, then out onto the stage, where he got somebody to put just a few of the stage lights on us, so we could feel the heat from them (they are hot). In the wings, he showed us the props and where the performers would wait before making their entrance. Backstage, we visited the makeup and costume departments and downstairs the dressing rooms, where Marc introduced us to Morgan Pearse, a member of the cast. "Are you the people I saw in the upper circle?" he asked. Indeed, we were, we informed him. "Have you been to the Opera before?" he enquired. "No, never" I replied. "Well, I hope you enjoy it" he said with a smile. "I'm sure we will. I'll look out for you." I said and he smiled as he dashed off to get ready. As it happened, I didn't have any trouble working out which one was him, he was playing Figaro … the lead character! I hope he wasn't offended as it was quite obvious we knew absolutely nothing about Opera.

I have to say though, we really enjoyed it. I think it helped that this production was in English, as we were able to follow the whole story, including the tricky bits when the surtitles that Marc had told us about appeared (they're like subtitles but on a screen above the stage). He joined us when we met Jane for supper at Browns after the show. It was great to be able to catch up and say thank you properly. A lovely end to a lovely evening with lovely people. Thanks buddy.

Chapter Thirty-Three
(25th October 2015)

Complete the Monopoly Board Challenge

I think everybody must have played Monopoly at some point in their lives. It's such a traditional family board game, I imagine most households have one. According to Wikipedia, it was first commercially sold in the 1930s and has become part of popular world culture, locally licensed in more than one-hundred-and-three countries and printed in more than thirty-seven languages. We own several versions; an early pre-1950s version that belonged to my Grandparents with cardboard playing pieces, a modern version which uses a debit card to complete your financial transactions and a worldwide version with landmarks from around the globe (which Josh took to Uni). In fact, these days there are so many variations, you can even have your own bespoke one made but I think most of us are familiar with the conventional one based on London.

It's not an original idea but haven't you always dreamt of visiting all the places on a Monopoly board? I know I have and as we were staying in London, after the Opera, what better time to do it. It looks so simple on the board doesn't it but I did some research on the internet and it's not quite as straight forward as it looks. There are lots of forums, where people say what they think is the best way around but there is no definitive route and it is certainly NOT a case of following the order on the board. So, in the end, I ignored what everybody else had said, printed off a map which someone had conveniently tagged the Monopoly place names on and decided to use the Citymapper app and Maps on our iPhones to work out the best way to get from one to another (thank heavens for modern technology).

We'd be starting from our hotel in Shepherds Bush and finishing at Victoria station, ready to catch our 6pm coach home. Some places were close together, others miles apart. We took a photo to record the time we reached each place on the board. There were a few occasions when poetic licence was required but basically our route went something like this;

10:22 Thames Water Tower (Water Works)
10:44 Park Lane
11:03 Mayfair
11:56 Bond Street
12:03 Oxford Street
12:03 Regent Street
12:07 Marlborough Street
12:24 Vine Street
12:24 Piccadilly
12:28 Pall Mall
12:37 Trafalgar Square
12:39 Whitehall
12:43 Northumberland Avenue
12:44 Strand
13:14 Fleet Street
13:27 Bow Street
13:39 Leicester Square
13:42 Coventry Street
14:05 Marylebone Station

14:36 Euston Road
14:59 King's Cross Station
15:06 Pentonville Road
15:20 Angel Islington
15:45 Liverpool Street Station
15:59 Whitechapel Road
16:27 Fenchurch Street Station
17:06 EDF Energy (Electric Company)

If you're wondering what we did for Chance and Community Chest; we bought a lottery ticket for the first and Mr C took a picture of my cleavage for the second and with regard to the Taxes ... we didn't pay them!

It took us just under seven hours and we covered twenty-three miles. There was only one property on the board that we didn't get to because it was south of the river, not easily accessed on public transport and unfortunately we just ran out of time. Which means one day we're going to have to "Go back to Old Kent Road"!

Chapter Thirty-Four

(26th October 2015)

Buy something at an auction

I've never actually been to a proper auction, I suppose partly because I've never had any real need to. My Mum and Dad used to go to auctions quite a bit. Dad was an electrician by trade then he and Mum moved into property development. As a child, growing up in Berkshire, we used to live in their "projects". The first was a shell, which they bought from the builder, then finished themselves. From there we moved to older properties that were in need of renovation. We would live in them while they were being modernised, then they'd be sold and we'd move on to the next one. I never knew quite what to expect when they said, "Come and have a look at our new home".

On one particular occasion we arrived at an old house and as Dad went to open the door, he calmly said "Mind your step as you go in". A sound warning indeed because as you stepped over the threshold, into the hallway, there were quite a few floorboards missing. Ah, home sweet home! Dad continued to do his contract work and Mum helped out, doing the general running around, collecting and delivering supplies, etc. At the same time, the house was being refurbished, with us living in it as it was being transformed into a nice family home. They bought another house a couple of doors down. We didn't live in that one, they converted it into two flats and Mum started managing the rental. This obviously proved lucrative because after a while, the decision was made to convert our house into two flats too, increasing their rental portfolio. A shower room was built under the stairs, a kitchen installed upstairs and the staircase was blocked off. We lived downstairs most of the time, although I do remember having to go out through the back door and in through the front door to go to bed upstairs in the transitional period.

I particularly liked our next home. We moved out of town a bit, into a big old gabled house with an orchard in the back garden and a paddock at the far end. It sounds very grand but of course, when we moved into it - it wasn't. It needed a lot of work, both inside and out. My Grandad was enlisted to help in the garden, chopping down trees that were either far too big or far too close to the back door. The paddock was completely overgrown and full of ant hills, so several chicken coops were built and attached to substantial runs, which were created using scaffolding poles and chicken wire. Then the hens arrived to help clear the land. We had two or three dozen Rhode Island Reds, who were prolific layers, so we'd sell excess eggs to the shop next door. There was also one black hen, which was my pet. I called her Cindy and I would carry her around with me all the time, pushing her about the orchard in my doll's pram, always watching for when she went into the nesting box to lay, so that I could eat "her" eggs. We had a couple of guinea fowl too, who would make a right old racket, like tin cans being rattled together, shouting a warning when they sensed danger. Sadly, they didn't always sense danger and towards the end of our time in this property, a fox got into the runs one night and killed the lot. It was a complete bloodbath!

Speaking of baths, when Dad took the old bath out of this house, he sank it into the ground down by the paddock, turning it into a pond. I'd go onto the Common to collect newts and frog spawn to populate it ... in the days when you were allowed to do that. We'd end up with hundreds of tadpoles. As they turned into tiny froglets, I would build little ramps, so they could climb out of the slippery sides of the bath and then the lawn would be awash with these tiny creatures, pinging through the grass. We had a big old shed, lined with racks, where we would store the apples harvested from the orchard in the autumn and a lean-to on the back of the shed, where we kept the grain for the chickens. You had to remember to shake the sack before scooping out the feed, as there were often mice feasting in there and they'd rush up your arm in a bid to escape if you startled them. The garden was lined with huge laurel hedges, which were so old that, if you could find your way in, once inside it was quite bare and great for making dens. It was a child's paradise in so many ways.

Indoors, the remodelling was well under way. Walls were going up and coming down. By Christmas, the door to Mum and Dad's room had been bricked up and the only way in was via a hole in the wall, where Dad had knocked through from the old bathroom, which had a considerably lower floor level than the bedroom. I have vivid memories of climbing up through the makeshift doorway, dragging my stocking behind me that year.

Unfortunately, whilst living there, we were burgled a couple of times. The first time they pinched a load of lead, used for the roof. A lad from the community of travellers, living on the common at that time, was responsible. The police caught him and it went to court. At the end of the hearing, as Dad was walking out, the lad's father took out a huge wad of bank notes and paid Dad the damages in cash in a "no hard feelings" kind of way. The second time we weren't so lucky. I was on a school trip to France and Mum and Dad had gone away for a few days. Someone broke in and stole everything, including all the jewellery my Grandad had made for my Mum over the years, smashing everything up and vandalising the house. Sadly, nothing was ever recovered. Not long after that the decision was made to move to Somerset. Dad's business partner had already moved his family down there and together, they were beginning to build houses, doing some of the work themselves and subcontracting the rest. They were building a development of five properties in North Perrott, so the plan was to sell four of them and for us to move into the fifth.

By the time we'd sold up and were ready to move, none of the new builds were complete. Finishing the houses which were due to go on the market took priority of course. As ours was still just a shell, Mum and Dad bought a big six berth caravan, parked it in the back garden, connected power and water … and that's where we lived for the first six months. There was one thing that was working in the new house - the toilet, so we weren't completely without facilities. As a child I thought it was fun living in a caravan on a building site … even though it was the long hot summer of 1976!

They continued to buy plots of land to develop, often at auction but I was always too young to attend. Now was the time to put that right. Not that I was going to buy a plot of land. I wasn't really looking for anything in particular, I just wanted the experience of bidding on something.

Pam and Joe suggested the Pump House Auctions, not too far from where we live. They hold regular sales, so I picked a date and called in on my way home from work a few days before, to pick up a catalogue and view the contents. There was all sorts of stuff, from antiques and jewellery to general tat. Pam and Joe said it was more of a house clearance sale than a quality auction but I had nothing to compare it with and found a couple of bits that I thought may be of interest. On the day of the auction, they met me there to show me the ropes. They decided there wasn't much that interested them and left early but I stayed to the end. I bid on a few things, losing a couple but winning a couple too. There was a small Railway sign, which Joe had expressed an interest in. I thought it would make a suitable gift as we'd arranged to have dinner with them the following day, to tell them all about our recent trip to Venice. I also bought a nice little chest, which looked like it had been used as a theatrical prop at some point in its life. I'm not sure I got a particularly great deal on it and I wasn't sure what I was actually going to do with it, I just liked it. Perhaps I could use it to store my Bucket List memorabilia in?

Chapter Thirty-Five

(3rd November 2015)

Walk to Winchester *(from home!)*

For some reason, Fi and I had been talking about walking to Winchester for ages. We'd often go for bimbles locally along the bridle paths to the shore and back across the cliffs (which are actually only small hills), around the common, down to the foreshore or along the River Hamble but said we really should think about doing something longer. We'd toyed with walking to Southampton and then Winchester came into the mix. As we'd never got any further than talking about it, once again we decided if I put it on the List, we'd do it. In our minds, we envisaged a nice route along the disused railway line from Wickham and through the Meon Valley but when we looked into it, that wouldn't actually take us anywhere near Winchester and the main idea was to walk to a destination that we could catch a train home from. Although a picturesque walk through the countryside would have been nice, as long as we were strolling and chatting it didn't really matter how rural our route was. So, we adjusted our plans and decided to walk to Winchester along the country roads (not via the motorway, obviously).

We picked a date that worked for both of us and although the weather forecast wasn't great, we thought we'd go for it anyway. We took waterproofs, just in case and if the weather really turned against us, we could always get a lift or a taxi, since we were never going to be that far from home. I got to Fi's house for 8.30am and we set off. Most of the way we were walking on pavements, although some bits were on the road and the last stretch, once we'd passed under the M3, was through countryside. It was a weekday and not during rush hour so, apart from the first bit, we didn't encounter much traffic. Not that that would have deterred us. I think we put the world to rights that day, talking about pretty much everything and everyone. We made a couple of refreshment stops along the way, trying not to linger for too long (which was always tempting). Despite our best efforts, by the time we reached Winchester we ended up having to catch a train home during the rush hour that we'd hoped to avoid. Nonetheless, we had finally got around to doing something we'd talked about for a couple of years and my diary entry for that day read *"Very excited to have completed another thing on the Bucket List - walk from Titchfield Common to Winchester, with the lovely Fi. The hilarious thing is, we cannot for the life of us remember why we were so excited about walking to Winchester in the first place! Anyhow, nearly nineteen miles in six hours (excluding stops for tea and cake in Botley and lunch at Fair Oak) and it's mission accomplished. We had a little bit of drizzle from time to time but luckily the rain at home never caught up with us. Very nice chap took a picture of us at Winchester Cathedral at the end of our walk ... although sadly managed to chop off the top of the magnificent building!!! Great day out and a great opportunity for a good natter ... believe it or not we DIDN'T run out of things to say!"*

True friendship. ♥♥♥

Chapter Thirty-Six

(23rd November 2015)

Send a message in a bottle

I love the romantic idea of finding a message in a bottle, washed up on the shore and I thought that sending one for my Bucket List would be a great idea. Living by the sea, it would be very easy but then, if anyone did ever find it, the likelihood is that it would be someone local. So I thought it would be nice to send one during our travels. Our trip to Antigua with Debbi and Morgan seemed the perfect destination. I printed off my message before we left home and included my email and postal addresses in the hope that somebody would respond. This is what I wrote;

November 2015

My name is Lesley Charlton. I was born in 1965 and turned 50 this year. To celebrate, I made a Bucket List of 50 things to do, one of which was to send a message in a bottle. If you find this message I would love it if you would send me an email/postcard saying where you found it, write your name and date on the back of this message, then pop it back in the bottle and toss it into the sea to hopefully continue its travels. Let's see how far it can travel.

Thank you for being a part of my Bucket List!

I thought about what type of bottle to use. Traditionally it would be a glass bottle but there is always the chance of that getting broken, so I decided to opt for a plastic bottle (although now I realise, with all the publicity about plastic pollution, this was a poor choice). The trouble was, I didn't want it to look like a piece of rubbish, so I put some brightly coloured glittery ribbon inside and tied colourful streamers to the top (not trashy at all!!!). Now, all I had to do was decide where and when to throw it in the sea.

As we were doing lots of diving, we had plenty of opportunities. The Caribbean Sea can be quite calm and I wanted to give it the chance to travel, so I took advice from our dive guides and the boat crew, who suggested a spot en-route to a particular dive site called Morgan's Anchor, south of our resort in Dickenson Bay. My message in a bottle was in my kit bag and ready to go. Out on the ocean, I crossed my fingers and Mr C filmed as I tossed it out into the foaming waters, created by the powerful motors of our dive boat. We watched it bob about as we sailed away.

Who knows if it will ever be found? It may end up with all the other rubbish in the oceans of the world, although I sincerely hope I haven't added to that. Sadly, nothing to report at the time of going to print but I hope that one day, somewhere, someone will find it and take the time to let me know.

Stranger things have happened, as this book testifies!

Chapter Thirty-Seven

(27th November 2015)

Go on a ghost walk

A Ghost Walk was one of the things that Debbi had on her Bucket List too, so it seemed silly not to do it together. Lots of cities do them and Portsmouth is full of history and ghostly tales, so we thought we'd stay local. A company called Dark Encounters were offering a Spice Island Ghost Walk;

Dark Encounters operate a guided tour around the seriously spooky Spice Island, mixing titbits of local history with some bloodcurdlingly gruesome tales of murder and even 18th century terrorism. The guides take you through 900 years of horrible history, making these walks as fascinating as they are frightening. You never know, a phantom sailor could stagger into your path in the ancient alleyways or a luminous figure hanging from the seaward side of the Round Tower may appear. What makes the tour so special is the visit to the Round Tower, normally off limits to the public. As you walk around the fortification you can understand why - this place has an ambiance that is more than a little eerie. Built in around 1418 to defend Portsmouth Harbour from French ships (the city had been attacked too many times during the Hundred Years War), the Tower is packed full of history.

We looked at the available dates and one of them was the day after we got home from Antigua. Knowing how long-distance travel can play havoc with your body clock, we thought it would be a good idea to book this one. It would give us something to look forward to on our return and a reason to stay up late, to readjust to the time zone.

Debbi and Morgan picked us up but there had been a bad accident on the M27, causing long delays. We decided to change our route and go via the Gosport ferry. We called Dark Encounters to say we may be a bit late. They said they couldn't wait for us but that, by the time we got there, they shouldn't have gone too far and we'd easily find them. Once we reached Portsmouth Hard we jumped into a taxi, which dropped us off at the Square Tower in Old Portsmouth just as the gentleman, very much in character for the period, was doing his introduction. Of course, we got a bit of stick for being late arrivals and warned not to loiter behind, for fear the ghosts may get us!

It was a dark, cold and rainy night, a complete contrast to Antigua, which really set the scene. Roles were assigned to certain people. The first was "The Nose", an informant who was to keep a look out for mysterious goings on. They asked for volunteers and Mr C nudged Debbi forward just as everyone else took a step back … hers by default. The walk took us through a secret tunnel, so secret that in all the years we'd lived here we'd never noticed it, although, now we know it's there we can't miss it! Then, it was along the seafront to Spice Island. The cast, in period costumes, were very good and would appear and disappear, as if from nowhere, as the stories unfolded. It wasn't actually quite as spooky as we thought a Ghost Walk would be. We'd expected people to be leaping out of the shadows, making us jump but it was more an evening of historic tales, embellished with ghost stories. Nonetheless, it was a good giggle. We really enjoyed it but by the time it was over we were ready for a drink, so we popped into the Still and West for a little liquid refreshment before walking back to the Hard to catch the ferry home.

Remarkably, we were all feeling quite normal and not at all jet lagged. I think our ghostly experience worked its magic.

Chapter Thirty-Eight

(12th December 2015)

Take a trip on the Eurostar

In all the years it has been in operation, I have never taken a trip on the Eurostar, so another perfect entry to put on the agenda. We fancied a trip to Bruges, to visit the Christmas Markets for a few days. Looking for partners in crime, Debbi and Morgan were keen to join us. We looked into the logistics of starting in London but by the time you factor in rail travel and an overnight stay (if you want to catch an early train to make the most of your time on the continent), it just wasn't practical. We decided the best option would be to do the two-hour drive to Ashford in Big Bertha, our faithful old BMW who just eats up the miles. Booked on the 7.28am train, we needed to set off around the wonderfully sociable hour of 4.30am, collecting Debbi and Morgan en-route. That would give us plenty of time to find the pre-booked parking and get checked in half an hour beforehand as requested.

Despite the early start, we were all very excited, chattering away as we began our journey. There was nothing on the roads and we were confident that we'd make good time. We'd just joined the A3, when a warning light came on in the car. She was an old girl, who'd had a few electrical issues in her life. Some warnings would disappear as quickly as they appeared, some were more sinister. The warning light soon went out. "I'll keep an eye on it" said Mr C casually. Just as we were approaching Queen Elizabeth Country Park, the light came on again and suddenly she lost all power. The engine was still running but when you put your foot on the accelerator ... nothing! Luckily, we were travelling downhill and there was a big lay-by, that truck drivers sometimes use for overnight stops, coming up. Mr C coasted down the road and parked up, knowing that sometimes, if you turned her off and on again (sound KC The Gadget Man advice), she would re-set herself. He tried that ... she didn't! We sat for a few minutes, then he tried again. Still nothing. Not to worry, we had time to spare and we had a breakdown recovery policy - at this time of day they shouldn't be busy. As I phoned through, we decided the best thing to do was get them to relay us to Ashford, so we could make the trip, then sort the car out when we got back. The RAC man came on the line and I explained our predicament. He sympathised but said it could be up to an hour before someone was with us. By the time the mechanic had assessed the situation and called for a pickup truck to transport us, we wouldn't make it.

We logged the job anyway, while we considered our alternatives. A taxi to Ashford would be ridiculously expensive and we'd still have to get home. Harvey the Hyundai was on the driveway at home but Josh was away at Uni, so couldn't bring it to us. Luckily Debbi and Morgan's car was on their driveway and their children, Maisie and Sam, were both at home that night. Neither were insured to drive the family car but they both had cars of their own. We decided the best option was to get them to come and collect Morgan, in one of their cars, take him home to collect his car, then he would come back to get us and we'd be on the road again. We did the maths and decided we should still be able to make it in time. An SOS call was made to the kids and they came out together, one driving while the other was on the phone, so we could talk to them to explain exactly where we were. In the meantime, I called the RAC man again, to inform him of our change of plan. We made arrangements to leave our ignition key on the front tyre, for somebody to come and collect Bertha and deliver her to our local garage. All we could do now was wait.

Maisie and Sam arrived quickly (I don't want to think about how quickly), picked Morgan up and headed for home – although, as it's a dual carriageway, they had to continue further up the A3 before they could turn around. We were able to track Morgan, via the Find My Friends app, which meant, as it was a cold night, we could sit in Bertha while we were waiting. When we knew he was getting close, we were ready. Flinging our cases in the boot, we leapt into the car and we were off.

It was just after 5.15am so, by our calculations, it was still doable. The atmosphere was tense. Debbi and I sat in the back so we couldn't see the speedo! As we monitored our progress, it looked like we were going to get there in time, which meant we could all relax a bit. At 6.29am we were on the M20 and on schedule to arrive at 7am. It was all looking so good ... until the motorway signs lit up, saying "Accident - Road Closed - 20-minute delay" and we came to a complete halt, engines off! We could not believe our bad luck, we'd got so close to making it, only to fall at the final hurdle. Debbi started making calls to Eurostar, seeing if there was any way we could change to another train but at that time in the morning, the office was closed. Resigned to the fact that we weren't going to get there in time (because even if we made it to Ashford, we still had to park the car), we knew we'd have to find another way of getting to Bruges.

We decided our best option was a ferry from Dover, then we could pick up a train in Calais. We'd still be able to return on the Eurostar, then get a taxi from Ashford back to wherever we'd left the car in Dover. We'd still get to Bruges, just a little later than planned. At 6.44am the traffic started moving again, slowly at first, then we began to pick up speed. Almost immediately, we passed the accident, which actually turned out to be a vehicle that had broken down in the outside lane, meaning they had to close the road temporarily to move it over to the hard shoulder. If we'd been there a couple of minutes earlier, we'd have avoided it!

Tension mounted as, once again, there was an outside chance we could make it. Nobody said much, as we wanted Morgan to concentrate on the road. We were almost there, we could see it … and then … we took a wrong turn. Mr C navigated us back on track and we arrived at the terminal at 7.14am. We could see the signs for our car park, so the boys dropped us girls and the luggage at the entrance and sped off to park the car. Debbi and I ran, as fast as we could with all the bags and arrived puffing and panting at the check-in desk, babbling about what a nightmare journey we'd had and explaining that our husbands were just a few minutes behind us so please, please would they let us on? "Oh, don't worry" said the laid-back young lady "We're not busy at this time of day, so there's no rush". No rush!

Did she have any idea what we'd been through to get here? The boys arrived in an equally flushed state, with just ten minutes to spare before departure but we'd made it.

We collapsed in the seating area to catch our breath, saying how amazing it was that we'd actually done it and re-living the ridiculous chain of events from the morning. It then dawned on us that, although we were in the waiting area, no announcements were being made. We looked at the information boards and realised we should already be on the platform. Grabbing our bags, we dashed off again and managed to clamber aboard, less than a minute before departure. As the train pulled away, we slumped into our seats and burst into a fit of nervous/exhausted laughter. By 7.33am we all had a glass of Prosecco in our hand ... and boy did we need it!

The rest of the weekend was very calm by comparison. Bruges was decorated for the festive season and looked so pretty. We visited the Christmas markets, which were small but enjoyable, we took a canal boat trip and did some beer sampling ... LOTS of beer sampling. We met up with Tamara, Mark and PJ, who are Belgian friends of Debbi and Morgan's. They live in Mechelen but Tamara was brought up in Bruges. They took us to places that only the locals know about, like Belgian Beer Pub Don Quichotte which, although it's right in the centre of the city, has an entrance that is so well hidden, you just wouldn't notice it. But our favourite was Brugs' Beertje, a hostelry whose menu listed over four-hundred beers. After asking us what we'd liked and disliked about the beers we'd tried already, Mark ordered for us and I have to say, his choices were spot on.

On our last day, we left our luggage in the lockers at the station, while we visited the Ice Sculpture Festival close by. Debbi made sure we were on a train that would get us back to the Eurostar terminal in time. In fact, we were there in PLENTY of time ... a full two-and-half hours before we were due to depart! Somehow, she'd got the maths wrong but it wasn't all her fault, none of us questioned her timings and at least we weren't going to be late!

The return journey went smoothly, both by Eurostar and car. Driving back down the A3, we looked over at the lay-by to see if Bertha was still there. Luckily, she wasn't. She'd been delivered safely to the garage and was eventually repaired. As for the Eurostar, well, I'm glad I did it but I can't say I'd rush to do it again. I don't know what I was expecting but at the end of the day, it's just a train. A fast one ... but still just a train. I guess if we lived closer to London, or Ashford, we'd consider it but it's not particularly convenient for us, especially as Southampton Airport is just fifteen minutes down the road.

Chapter Thirty-Nine

(1st January 2016)

Plan someone else's 50th Birthday

Knowing how long these things take, we'd been asking Colin what he wanted to do for his fiftieth birthday for ages. "Oh, I don't know" he'd say, to which our reply would be "Well if you don't plan something soon, we'll plan it for you" and he'd just tut and say he'd think about it. It was New Year's Day and we were all feeling pretty mellow, after our Venetian Mask themed New Year's Eve party the night before. Deb, Colin, Keith and Sara had stayed over and Debbi and Morgan had returned, under the pretence of collecting their car, for lunch. It was a bit of a duvet day, lighting the log burner and staying in our pyjamas (not Debbi and Morgan of course). Again, we asked Colin the question and again he gave the same reply. "Come on Colin" we cajoled him "it's the start of the year and you're going to be fifty, so let's get it sorted" but he just shrugged and smiled. We started questioning about things he might like to do. A party was definitely out but going somewhere and doing something was definitely in.

We pointed out that, as luck would have it, this year his birthday was just a few days before Easter and the following week formed part of the Easter Holidays, a perfect time to go away with a group of friends … hint, hint. Incorporating the Bank Holiday weekend meant people wouldn't have to take so many days leave and the Easter Break meant that, should anybody be working in education ... wink, wink (Deb and Keith) ... they wouldn't be teaching. A group holiday with friends, he was starting to nod his head, this was beginning to look promising. "But who would you want to take with you?" we asked, not putting him on the spot at all but all smiling in his direction. "Well, you lot I suppose, if you want to come" and in unison everybody said, "Yes we'll come", startling him with our exuberant response. Brilliant. All we had to do now was find somewhere to go. It needed to be in the UK really as, with it being Easter and just three months away, we'd probably left it too late to get reasonably priced flights abroad.

Mr C and I talked about the barn conversion in Devon that we'd booked a few years ago, for our family to spend Christmas together. There were ten of us, aged three to eighty-three, making our own entertainment, sitting together around the big farmhouse table and taking trips to the beach, even when it was blowing an absolute hoolie. It was like an episode of The Waltons (showing my age) but we all had a fabulous time. I guess we painted such a fantastic picture that everyone was nodding in agreement, saying something like that would be just great.

So, the initial criteria was set:
1) somewhere in the West Country (at least as a starting point)
2) a minimum of four double bedrooms (none of this sofa-bed malarkey)
3) a large kitchen-diner with a table that would seat us all, to maximise our socialising area

These were deemed the essential points, so the search began. Our Mac is in the conservatory and ideal for mass viewing of the internet. Mr C was on it and when he found a property that ticked all the boxes, he'd pull up the photos and we'd all lean in for a closer look, passing comments as he flicked through the images. There were a few "possibilities" and a lot of "definitely nots" along the way … and then we found it!

This large, semi-detached, period farmhouse sits on the owners' working sheep farm, close to the village of Whitstone, near the stunning coast of North Cornwall. Tucked away in an idyllic, rural setting and surrounded by acres of countryside, this Cornish farmhouse provides spacious holiday accommodation for a family reunion in a warm and welcoming period property.

Complete with a friendly farmhouse pub next door, which is open evenings only and mainly used by locals, this cottage offers traditional features, including slate floors and wooden beams, coupled with contemporary luxury.

It has a large kitchen-diner and sitting room. On the first floor, you will find five bedrooms (three with en-suite facilities) and a family bathroom. The spacious, private garden will be adored by all the family, with large, enclosed lawns. Use of a children's play area and small fishing lake stocked with carp and tench on the neighbour's land and an attached pub offering a friendly atmosphere for refreshment, chatting with the locals, or a quiet game of pool.

Less than half an hour's drive from the popular surf at Widemouth Bay, just a little south of Bude. Along with the beautiful beaches, there are some quaint coastal villages to visit including pretty Port Isaac and charming Clovelly, with its cobbled street running down to the sea. Whether you wish to surf, walk, fish or simply relax in the outdoors, this country cottage in Cornwall is sure to appeal.

Note: Unfenced duck pond at front

Everybody was nodding excitedly as Mr C read the description. It seemed a perfect fit. It was available for the week we wanted and reasonably priced, so we booked it there and then. Job done, Colin leant back in his chair with a sigh. Oh dear, had we got over enthusiastic and bullied him into it? Luckily not, he was just glad that we'd finally get off his case about planning his big birthday.

I was nominated as the Party Planner (Bucket List - tick) and over the next few weeks, produced a brochure, detailing the proposed programme of events (although these plans are always fluid and subject to change if we find something better to do):

Saturday 26th March
Rendezvous Chez Charlton 10am
Lunch around 1pm en-route
Supermarket delivery late pm
Check out the pub next door
Light supper and games

Sunday 27th March
Easter Egg Hunt and Easter Craft
Orientation and trip to the seaside
Roast Dinner

Monday 28th March
Trip to Clovelly
Find some oysters for Colin to try
Pub games tournament next door

Tuesday 29th March
Murder Mystery

Wednesday 30th March
Bude Brewery Tour by minibus
Pantyhose Bowling

Thursday 31st March
(Colin's Official Birthday)
Tintagel
Lunch out somewhere
Party food and party games - Theme "Black"

Friday 1st April
April Fools jokes

Saturday 2nd April
Stop for Fish & Chips at Lyme Regis on the way home

Fast forward now, to the beginning of Colin's Birthday celebrations.

Saturday - We rendezvoused at ours as planned, loaded our luggage into two cars and set off - boys in one car (to play Pub Cricket of course) and girls in another. As tradition dictates, when travelling in a group to the West country, we stopped off at The Red Lion in Babcary for lunch, then it was onwards to our final destination. Arriving in good time, we met with the owner who showed us around. The farmhouse wasn't exactly as we'd imagined. The kitchen-diner was going to be perfect as a central hub but the lounge, to us, felt a little like the communal area of a retirement home. However, overall the accommodation was ideal for what we had planned. We unpacked and then the girls set about decorating the Easter Tree, which took pride of place on the dining room table, while we waited for our grocery delivery to arrive. Once the consignment of essentials was received and stored, we settled in with a light supper and a toast to the start of the festivities.

Sunday – Being Easter Sunday everyone dressed for breakfast in either Easter Bonnets or Bunny Ears then, swapping our headwear for something a little more practical, we set off for our trip to the seaside. We drove to Widemouth Bay, where we parked up and set off on a scenic walk to Bude. Although it was blustery, the skies were blue and the boys were able to burn off some energy, running around and balancing on boulders, as we bimbled along the clifftop. Arriving in Bude, we were all in agreement that it was pasty o'clock. After perusing a few outlets, we chose Pengenna Pasties to make our purchase, where the pasties were huge! After a meal of such substance we were in need of liquid refreshment and spotted The Globe Hotel, which looked like it could provide what we were seeking. Being in the West Country, what better way to quench your thirst than with a nice pint of cider. Choosing to sample something local, we discovered a new favourite ... Rattler Cloudy Cornish Cyder. In fact, it was so popular that, as the designated drivers, Keith and I left the others in the bar (just to make absolutely sure they liked the Rattlers), while we went to retrieve the vehicles, thus avoiding a potentially wobbly stagger back along the cliffs for some. As it was about an hour's walk back to the cars and we were planning a roast for supper, we decided to save time and take a taxi back to the car park at Widemouth Bay. We paid our fare and got out. Looking around, we couldn't see either of our cars ... and then we realised, we didn't actually recognise the car park. Walking up onto higher ground, we spotted a second car park at the far end of Widemouth Bay. Laughing at our rookie error, we took a brisk walk along the coastal path, to find both cars exactly where we'd left them. After a quick swoop back through Bude to collect the rabble, it was a short drive home to the farmhouse. Despite being a few ciders down, the boys cooked a splendid roast, with all the trimmings, for supper while the girls set about marbling hard-boiled eggs with food colouring (Easter craft) and had a good old boogie to some classic tunes, supplied by DJ Kevvy Kev.

Monday – An outing to the lovely Clovelly. Having parked at the top of the village we were guided by the whiff of donkey as we made our way down the steep, cobbled main street, which is lined with architecturally listed, chocolate box beautiful cottages, all the way to the harbour. Unfortunately, just as we got there, a squall came through and the only place to shelter was in the pub … oh well … when needs must! Once the rain abated, we took a stroll along the harbour wall, before beginning our ascent for the return journey. Walking back up through the village, we stopped off at The Cottage Tea Rooms. Most of the boys continued the pursuit of their self-imposed pasty a day quest, while Keith joined the ladies in a cream tea. Despite the short blip in the weather, we'd had a lovely trip to this picture-postcard pretty village. The journey home was filled with excitement for the Easter Egg Hunt, which had been postponed from the day before. Secreted around the farmhouse were a selection of eggs, including plastic ones which contained either chocolate mini eggs or jigsaw pieces (parts of larger puzzles). Deb and Colin won the grand prize of the chocolate bunny for the most eggs collected, although when we started putting together the jigsaws, it became obvious that a couple of the eggs were missing. Unfortunately, Mr C and I had crept down the night before and hidden so many that we'd forgotten where we'd put them all and despite a second, very detailed, search they could not be located. (Throughout the rest of the week, people would randomly check a cubby hole that they thought may have been overlooked, in an attempt to find the missing eggs but to no avail. Ironically, they came to light when nobody was actually looking for them, on the day we checked out!). The pub games, scheduled for the evening, were replaced with a very grown-up game of Pie Face, although ours was the cheaper version called Splat, which had a pathetically weak mechanism that struggled to cope with launching the large dollop of frothy cream into the face of the, supposedly, unsuspecting victim. It created a lot of laughs but not really for the right reasons.

Tuesday (which happened to be my birthday) - Supplies had been running low but we hadn't wanted to waste our time grocery shopping, so another on-line order had been placed for delivery later in the day, when we knew we'd be home getting ready for our Murder Mystery evening (details in Chapter 23 if you've forgotten). This left the daytime free to explore, so we decided to start with a trip to Bodmin Jail. The weather was cold and damp, which added to the atmosphere as we explored each floor of the gloomy prison, that nearly gained another inmate … when we almost lost Debbi, during a slight mix-up with regard to which "Deb" was being referred to, which went something like this; While descending a steep, narrow, spiral staircase after exiting a warren of cells, someone at the front called out "Has anyone got Deb?" and someone else replied "Yes, she's with me.". However, when we got to the bottom, we realised that nobody actually did have Deb (Debbi) and she'd been left on a completely different floor. Discovering our mistake, she was soon collected and very glad to be repatriated with the group. On our way home, we stopped off at Port Isaac. Not realising how pretty it was there, we'd only paid for an hour in the car park, when actually two would have been better. Nonetheless, we managed to fit in pasty number three (steak and stilton, which was documented in my diary as *"the best yet"*) and some Cornish Saffron Cake (because everyone should have cake on their birthday). Back at the ranch, it was time to prepare for our Murder Mystery evening and the ensuing confusion for the poor delivery man as detailed earlier.

Wednesday – Unfortunately, forces out of our control conspired against us and we had been unable to arrange a tour of the Bude Brewery but as we'd already been to Bude and discovered Rattlers, we decided to have a play-day at the farmhouse instead. Sara had bought cardboard light sabres, filled with chocolate eggs, for the boys. Eggs removed, an epic Star Wars battle commenced! It was all getting a bit rambunctious, so we decided to take a selection of outdoor games up to the field, where there was much more space for those boisterous boys to let off steam. Subsequently, the afternoon was a relaxed affair of films and books (in the waiting-to-die lounge). In the evening, we popped to the pub next door, which was a strange little place, with an even stranger selection of clientele. It had a pool table ... but not a lot of atmosphere, so we didn't exactly make a night of it there. After a mini pool tournament, with couples competing against each other to be crowned over-all winners, we returned to the farmhouse, for a much more sophisticated game of Pantyhose Bowling in the hallway. For those unfamiliar with this cultured activity, you put a one leg of a pair of tights inside the other, to form a stronger receptacle, insert a tennis ball down into the toe piece, then take it in turn to put the gusset part of the tights on your head. With your hands behind your back, you lean forward and using a swinging motion, attempt to knock all the skittles (bottles of water) over as quickly as possible. The person who achieves the shortest time wins. It's what hallways are made for!

Thursday – the day we'd allocated as Colin's Official Birthday. At breakfast, Colin was crowned King for the Day, adorned with 50th Birthday badges and showered with gifts, before setting off to Tintagel Castle. Our Bertha was the thirstier of the two cars and the cheapest petrol was in the opposite direction, so the day before, I'd popped out early, to spend a swift eighty pounds filling her up. Loading the cars in preparation for our outing, there was a distinct whiff of fuel. We looked around but there was no evidence of a source, so the girls got in. When I started the engine, the fuel gauge was showing half a tank! Bemused, I turned the engine off and called the boys over. Although she was old, she had a locking petrol cap, so it was unlikely that someone had syphoned the fuel out. The boys walked around the car, administering the "sniff test". The smell was definitely strongest at the back, around the tank. Morgan ran his fingers underneath and discovered petrol on the <u>outside</u> – not good! On closer inspection, it became obvious that we had a leak, which had been masked by the fact that I had parked on gravel ... and directly over a drain. An added concern was that we were very close to the duck pond (as documented in the house description). Hoping the drain and the pond were not connected, we decided the best course of action was to make a hasty exit, head to Tintagel and try to find a garage. Somebody must have been looking after us that day because a splendid gentleman at Tintagel Motors identified the leak in the fuel tank, appreciated our predicament and said that if we could leave the car with him for the day, he'd see what he could do. At that point it was out of our hands and the only thing to do was enjoy Colin's birthday. The weather was glorious and by now everyone was feeling a bit peckish, so it was time for pasty number four (which we'd failed to achieve on our farmhouse day) before setting off to explore the castle. The lunch out that we'd planned turned into dinner at the King Arthur's Arms, waiting for our magical mechanic to patch the tank. Grateful that he'd got us back on the road, as we'd feared it may have brought our little holiday to an abrupt end on the back of a breakdown vehicle, we fully expected to have to pay an arm and a leg for such super service and were gobsmacked when the bill was just seventy pounds! What a superstar, although it did mean that, after such a long day, we'd run out of time and had to postpone poor Colin's birthday party.

Friday – Colin's Official Birthday Take Two ... and April Fool's Day! We were all very guarded when we got up, as everyone had planned a practical joke of some sort but didn't want to get caught out by anyone else. The two most successful pranks involved cars, which was rather topical considering the events of the previous day! A couple of days before our trip, Debbi and Morgan had bought a new car and it was Debbi's pride and joy ... so I'd arranged for Josh to call her, to tell her it had been stolen and involved in an accident. He had all the facts; make, model, registration number, her address and postcode, etc. The scene was set and just as we all sat down to breakfast, I texted Josh to signal it was time for him to call. He created a very convincing story, introducing himself as a police officer and confirming she was the registered owner of the vehicle, then explaining that some young lads had been driving the car at speed and lost control on a named road we are all familiar with, crashing into the traffic calming barriers. There were gasps and worried faces as everyone listened in to Debbi's side of the conversation, trying to piece together what had actually happened as she pressed "the policeman" for details. Nobody else was in on the gag, so they couldn't give it away and Josh managed to keep it going for long enough to make it uncomfortable (for everyone) but short enough that it didn't induce a nervous breakdown. He was brilliant ... and I think she's just about forgiven him! The other convincing caper was much simpler but just as effective. Morgan had placed a rather realistic sticker on Keith and Sara's offside rear wheel arch, making it look like all the paint had been scraped off. Nobody had noticed when we headed out for the day and by coincidence, Keith was driving the boys in their car as they lead the way, while Sara was in the front passenger seat of ours as I followed. At one point, it was a very tight squeeze when we had to pull into a passing place to let a very large vehicle through. Shortly after that, Keith was turning right, exposing the "massive scratch" just in front of us. Sara was convinced that it must have just happened during our close encounter with the oncoming truck. She was having a right old go at Keith (to us), accusing him of being distracted by the boys and that he couldn't have been concentrating as he would have felt the vehicle hit him. As soon as we parked at our destination, she was out of the car, quick as a flash and launching into a tirade of abuse at the poor, unsuspecting Keith, who stood with his mouth open, in utter confusion, as she went to inspect the "damage". Nice one Morgan! When she'd calmed down, all was forgiven. Continuing to check out the Cornish coast, our first port of call, or should I say harbour of call, was Boscastle. We strolled along the harbour wall, had a cream tea at The Bridge House and did a spot of retail therapy, to help calm the nerves of those affected by the April Fools japes. From there, we headed to Trebarwith Strand to play cricket on the beach, only by now the tide was in and the sand was submerged, leaving nothing exposed except the rocks at the base of the cliffs. Match abandoned, there was nothing else to do except console ourselves with a pint and a view from The Port William above the bay, before heading home for the party. What we didn't realise was that the boys had been up to more mischief. Whilst balancing on the rocks by the shore, Keith's mobile had slipped out of its case and landed in a rock pool! They'd fished it out as quickly as possible but the saltwater was giving it "issues", which they were all sworn to secrecy about for fear of Sara's recriminations as she had only just forgiven him for the "scratch" (although they were rumbled later that day when they were found trying to covertly dry it out on a radiator. Luckily, the phoned lived to fight another day … and Keith didn't get told off TOO much!). The theme for Colin's party was "Black" – his signature wardrobe colour. There were banners, balloons and poppers, party food with jelly and ice-cream and LOTS of games. Debbi was the "dolly doing her dealing" as we Played our Giant Cards Right and of course, a birthday party would not be complete without Pass the Parcel, only this time the parcel was wrapped in miles of clingfilm, to stop multiple layers being removed at once. As always, it brought out the worst in people, turning a simple children's' game into a full-on contact sport.

Saturday – Time to go home. We had to leave anyway, as there was no more room in the recycling bins for the bottles and cans! Also, we'd kept checking the ducks on the pond, who hadn't been exhibiting any obvious signs of petrol poisoning, as yet, so if we left now and they did become unwell, hopefully the finger of suspicion would not be pointed at us. We'd achieved most things on the agenda, although sadly Colin didn't get to try his oysters and we hadn't managed to eat a pasty EVERY day. Of course, a trip home from the West Country is NEVER complete without stopping off at Lyme Regis.

Lyme Regis is about 15 miles from Crewkerne where, as I said, I'd lived as a child and was often our seaside destination of choice at the end of the day. I have fond memories of warm summer afternoons playing on the beach, windswept blustery Sundays walking along The Cobb, hunting for fossils on Monmouth Beach, school friends' birthday parties (a mackerel fishing trip followed by an ice-cream cone), cockles and mussels from the seafood stall opposite the Cobb Arms and the best fish and chips in the whole wide world EVER from the chippy by the Lifeboat Station, which had to be eaten sitting on the sea wall. These are the delights that I am still on a mission to introduce to as many of my friends as possible.

The sun shone gloriously as we strolled along the Cobb and ate our fish supper. An idyllic end to our big birthday jaunt and the completion of my party planning challenge.

Chapter Forty
(15th January 2016)
Visit Lumiere London

Billed as the UK's largest Light Festival, Fi and Andy had visited the Lumiere in Durham and said it was well worth a look, so we were excited to learn that it was coming to London and would give us the perfect opportunity to spend a couple of days in the capital (as if we needed an excuse). Fi and I met at antenatal classes and subsequently became good friends, as part of the same First Time Mums group. Their daughter, Hannah, was in London working on a gap year with XLP and with Josh at Uni in Westminster, we could see the Lumiere and visit our fledglings at the same time. The added bonus was that it tied in nicely with Hannah's birthday. We collected Fi and Andy, parked at the train station and bought our tickets. Sipping Prosecco during our journey on the way up set the scene for a fun weekend ahead.

Josh met us at Victoria Station and we made our way to a nearby hostelry to wait for Hannah. It made my heart melt seeing our beautiful youngsters together again, so at ease in each other's company. Of course, they've known each other since they were born and as children it was a bit of a love/hate relationship as they were both big characters, extremely sociable but very strong willed. They spent a lot of time together before starting school, then education took them on separate paths but as Fi and I would meet up regularly, it was inevitable that they would continue to see each other too and over time, they developed a very special bond. Effortlessly slipping back into that friendship, they chatted animatedly and our joy swelled.

To celebrate Hannah's birthday, we'd made a table reservation on the South Bank for cocktails and supper later that evening. So, after planning where and when we'd all meet, we left them to it and headed off to drop our bags at our accommodation. Fi had found us a great deal for two nights at the Central City Road Travelodge, giving us a perfect base with easy access to all the things we were planning to do. We rendezvoused with the "kids" and their significant others at Giraffe, in time to take advantage of the Happy Hour Cocktails … only to find that Happy Hour does not apply on a Friday night! Oh well, it was Hannah's birthday and it was just nice spending the time together. Of course, we always knew that the evening was going to be courtesy of the banks of Mum and Dad. It was a lovely evening, full of lively chatter, good food, good company and a great birthday cake (Fi is the birthday cake Queen, although how she'd managed to transport this wonderful creation, intact, to its destination is beyond me). Not that the youngsters wanted to hang around with us oldies all night so, as they headed off to do their own thing, we decided to start checking out the Lumiere.

The festival was a series of eccentric creations of art, lighting up London in thirty locations, on some of the city's most iconic streets and landmarks. A mixture of 3D projections, interactive installations and illuminated artworks. It was a free event, on for four nights, running from the Thursday to the Sunday from 6.30pm to

10.30pm. We'd printed off a map, showing where each exhibit would be and decided to walk back via Westminster Abbey and Leicester Square as an introduction. Some exhibits were more spectacular than others (my diary entry, next to my picture of Westminster Abbey, read *"This one was spectacular ... others were not!"*) but the exhibitions certainly attracted a lot of interest. As advertised, at 10.30pm the lights went out and we made our way back to our hotel for a nightcap.

The following morning, after a leisurely brunch, we chose to travel into town by bus. Bagging the front seats on the top deck, we were like children on a school outing. We made our way back to Leicester Square to meet up with Hannah and James where, thanks to a friend of Fi's, we had complimentary tickets for the afternoon viewing of the new Star Wars film, being screened in the IMAX cinema. Josh had said that he didn't have to start work until later in the day and we managed to get an extra ticket for him to join us. It's amazing what you can achieve with a little bribery when your enthusiasm for spending time with your little munchkins is greater than their enthusiasm for spending time with you!

After the film, waiting for the Lumiere to light up again, we decided to install the boys in a pub while the girls had a wander along Oxford Street. Re-joining them a little later, we thought it would be sensible to get a bite to eat before we looked at the lights. Finding a table for seven (Josh had gone to work but we'd been joined by Fi's sister, Claire) early on a Saturday evening was not that easy though. We wandered around for a bit, without success, then ended up at a quirky little restaurant which, as it happens, was right opposite the pub we'd started at! They said they could open up a small seating area in their basement, which was perfect as we'd have it to ourselves. Josh's girlfriend worked close by, so when she finished her shift we invited her to join us too. The menu was eclectic but both the food and cocktails were good and it was reasonably priced - amazing for such a central location. We played Telestrations (a sort of Chinese whispers drawing game) very noisily, while waiting for another couple of Fi and Andy's friends to meet up with us, then set off to sample more of the Lumiere. My diary entry for that day read *"Again, some underwhelming but some really lovely"* which I think sums it up quite fairly. Don't get me wrong, we really enjoyed it but Fi and Andy agreed it wasn't as good as the one they'd been to in Durham.

Numbers had dwindled to our original party of four and we were at Oxford Circus when the lights were switched off, so decided to find a traditional pub for a traditional pint before heading back. Ale supped, we made our own entertainment, both waiting for and riding on the night bus home. By the time we were back at the hotel, none of us wanted to go to bed, so we took a bottle of wine to our room, to socialise a little longer. By 1am we'd got the munchies again and had a sudden yearning for a kebab - yes, they are firmly back on my menu these days. Checking out what was available locally on one of the numerous fast food apps, we discovered that Angel Kebab would deliver. Excitedly we phoned through our order and went downstairs to the Travelodge all-night bar to await its arrival. It was a classy place to be on a Saturday night, hosting an interesting bunch of characters. I've never seen so many tattoos and missing teeth ... and that was just the ladies! The people watching was fantastic, as was the kebab. Get us ... living the high life!

Sunday morning wasn't an early start but when we finally did get going we made our leisurely way back to Victoria Station, for a late lunch with Hannah and James before catching our train home. In the station car park, despite her ongoing intermittent issues, Bertha started up okay. We dropped Fi and Andy back, turning the engine off while they got their bags out and we said goodbye. However, as we went to leave, she would not start again. The battery appeared to be completely flat. So flat that we couldn't even jump start her from Andy's Merc. Tired from our weekend away we pushed her into a parking space and Andy drove us home, deciding to deal with the situation the following day. We had other cars in the fleet on our drive that we could use if we'd needed to.

In the morning I returned to Fi and Andy's and called the RAC. The gentleman arrived promptly. I told him the series of events leading up to the flat battery and he scratched his head. "Let's give it a go anyway" he said as he turned the key ... and Bertha started immediately. I apologised profusely for wasting his time. I hadn't even thought about trying to start her myself before calling him out. He wasn't at all bothered but could offer no explanation for what happened the night before. Ah, the anomalies that are our Bertha. Don't you just love a car with character?

Chapter Forty-One

(22nd January 2016)

Retire at Fifty

Who'd have thought I'd be able to put this one on the List! It was a nice idea but the chances were slim. It would be madness to walk away from the perfect job (flexible one day a week, term time only contract, running my own diary and not a bad pro-rata salary). Don't get me wrong, I loved my job and the people I worked with. I'd been a Schools Liaison Officer with the same college for over twenty years. It started after being made redundant while working in the financial services industry. We'd already talked about starting a family, so when my job ended, I wasn't that sad. Up until then we'd had a good joint income and great lifestyle but redundancy gave us the opportunity to see if it would be viable for us to survive on one salary as, ideally, I wanted to be a stay-at-home Mum.

A friend who worked at the job centre insisted I signed on for unemployment benefit while deciding what to do. I wasn't keen but she told me not to be so proud, pointing out that I'd always worked and paid into the system so was fully entitled to make a claim. Semi-reluctantly I did. In those days you had to prove you were looking for work but it wasn't as stringent as it is today. As evidence, I would collect newspaper cuttings of the jobs I'd applied for. Hoping I would be pregnant soon (at which point I would cease my claim), I tried to make sure that, when I submitted my CV, I was either under or overqualified for the position advertised. I didn't like wasting prospective employers' time but equally, I didn't want to take a job then promptly leave, so assumed that, by selecting jobs I wasn't quite right for, I'd get rejected on the first sift, keeping everybody happy. Generally, I'd get a response of "thanks but no thanks" (back in the day when you would actually get an acknowledgement when you submitted a job application), which of course was the reply I was hoping for.

One of the jobs I applied for was at a local College of Further Education. I got a nice letter back, saying I was overqualified for the post but that they would keep my details on file. A polite way of saying "no", I thought, particularly as I had no experience of working in education. To my surprise, some weeks later they got in contact with me, asking if I'd be interested in a short-term, part-time post to cover planned sick leave. I had literally just fallen pregnant with Josh and this sounded ideal, so I responded that indeed I was. My lack of knowledge of the schooling sector was apparently unimportant, as they'd picked up on the fact that I had produced and delivered marketing presentations in my financial services role and it was this that had drawn me to their attention. At interview, it was explained that they wanted somebody to hold the fort for the Schools Liaison Officer, who was off on planned sick-leave, which should be a pretty simple task as it wasn't term-time, so calls, emails and general liaising duties would be minimal. However, whilst doing this they wanted me to put together a presentation about the college that could then be taken out to schools at the start of the new academic year. The temporary contract was to cover the summer holidays but college staff would still be available, so I'd be able to talk to people in the different departments, finding out what they did and how they would like their subject areas promoted. It was two-and-a-half days a week for three months, which again was ideal. It meant I could attend all my antenatal appointments and nobody need even know I was pregnant. It wasn't as if I was going to be taken on permanently, as the lady whose role I was covering was due back at the end of the summer vacation. It was a win-win situation and I started straight away. I really enjoyed it, got to know lots of people and learnt lots about Further Education. My co-workers talked about the pressures of the job and the stresses of working to deadlines but neither of these things were anywhere near as bad as they had been working in Financial Services, which at the time was in the throes of super-strict legislation coming into force, so I actually found it refreshingly less fraught.

I fielded the work that came in to the Schools Liaison Office, did my research and wrote the marketing script, producing the presentation materials on a series of slides, with colourful text and lots of clip art ... all printed on acetates (oh, how things have moved on). Job complete, I was ready to do my handover. My manager, Hilary, took me aside and said that she was so impressed with what I'd done that she had managed to secure funding and was able offer me a permanent position! I was flattered but obviously it was a bit awkward. As much as I'd loved the people and enjoyed the job, I knew I didn't want to work once the baby was born. On top of that, I'd been discretely managing my pregnancy and nobody actually knew I was expecting. I thought the best course of action was to say that I couldn't accept her kind offer, as I already had plans to move my Mum and Dad back from Spain (true) and wasn't sure how long that was going to take (also true). She said she understood but was happy to wait! I was digging myself into a hole, so just had to come clean. Explaining the full situation, she thanked me for my honesty and asked if I'd be prepared to be kept on the books as a casual worker, in case they needed to call on me at any time. I was more than happy with that solution and was very grateful that she thought I was worth it.

As it happened, I did keep getting called back when they needed a spare pair of hands, both before and after Josh was born. I also stepped in to do a few weeks work when the lady I'd covered for before developed appendicitis on a cruise and had to be landed in France, unable to fly home until she had recovered. When she returned to work, she still needed assistance, so I started going in, on average, one day a week to help out. Sometimes I'd just pop in for a few hours at short notice, taking Josh with me, hanging him in his baby bouncer in my office doorway. Even the Principal would chat to him as she went past. It seemed to suit everybody. Sometime later, HR called me to a meeting to discuss the fact that I was casual labour. I thought they were going to say that there was no longer funding for occasional roles but instead, they said it would be in my best interest to sign a permanent contract, that way I would be covered for things like holiday and sick pay and I'd get paid at the end of the month, rather than submitting time sheets, meaning I was effectively getting paid two months in arrears. They agreed to my flexible working, so although a regular day was nominated, I could change which day I worked each week, to fit with both the workload and my other commitments. I could even work more than one day a week when it suited, accumulating hours to take off at a later date, which was useful as I couldn't take actual holiday in term time. Also, once Josh started school, I was able to finish early to pick him up. As long as I worked my total annual hours each academic year, they were happy. With this annualised term time contract in place, I had a regular monthly salary and all the school holidays off. Talk about falling in the proverbial pile of manure and coming up smelling of roses. Having said that, I was appreciative of my good fortune and did my very best to do a good job. I loved the role, could work it around Josh and had a bit of extra spending money. Life was good.

My contract remained the same for over twenty years. Other employees came and went but I was the constant in the Schools Liaison Department and therefore, in time, the main point of contact for the local schools. I was offered more hours but I didn't want them, particularly after Steve died and I was a single Mum. They'd been very generous with my compassionate leave too. When we were told by the Oncology Consultant there was nothing else they could do for Steve, we were also told that arrangements could be made for him to be cared for at home, where he wanted to be, until he died. I called my manager to say I didn't want to be at work as Steve only had "a few weeks to not many months" left and obviously I wanted to spend all that time with him. I said I was prepared to resign if need be but she told me to leave it with her and not make any decisions until she'd seen what arrangements could be made. A few days later, she visited me at home and told me HR would not accept my resignation and had put me on compassionate leave, for as long as I needed. How fantastic was that! Steve died in the April and I didn't return to work until the following September. For all the college's faults, of which there were many, I have nothing but gratitude for the way they looked after me during those difficult times.

Over the years the college went through many changes and restructures. Each time I wondered how it would affect me but each time I managed to slip through the net. I was told my job was "at risk" once, when they were trying to cut costs and reduce the head count. Someone looked at my job (on paper) and asked how a role like mine could be done in so few hours. Once I explained to my new manager what I did and how I did it, the threat of redundancy was quickly withdrawn. To my amusement, the higher echelons never really knew which department to put Schools Liaison in. It moved between Marketing and Client Services, a department which got rebranded a couple of times. As the years ticked by and the management structure changed, I just kept my head down and got on with it, obviously to a satisfactory level, so they pretty much left me to it.

In the summer of 2015, a shock announcement was made, about a week before the long holidays, that yet another restructure would take place. It was going to be a major shake-up, with lots of redundancies. I knew that this would usher in more big changes and new (although usually not so new) ideas about how to cut costs and improve productivity. I'd been around the block a few times now and wasn't sure if I could face "reinventing the wheel" again, so asked HR for a forecast of my redundancy payment so I could do the maths. When I returned to work in the September, the teaching staff were the only group of employees whose futures had been settled, everything else was still up in the air. It was chaotic. Department by department, they worked their way through the college, "reviewing" each role. When it got to my section, I was not at all surprised to be put "at risk" once again and was given a pack containing my financial entitlement, other jobs I could apply for and what to do if I wanted to appeal. Although I moaned about it sometimes, I loved my job, the people I worked alongside and the staff and pupils in the schools I dealt with but the college itself was changing beyond recognition. Morale was at an all-time low and I just didn't have the enthusiasm to fight for a role. Also, Josh was away at Uni, so I didn't need to be tied to an academic calendar anymore and I was trying to help Mr C, such as I could, develop his business. Decision made, I requested a meeting with my manager and the head of HR and asked if I could save them all time by requesting voluntary redundancy. They encouraged me to look more closely at one of the other jobs on offer but it was more hours, more responsibility and quite frankly more trouble than it was worth. Thanking them for their consideration, I stuck to my guns and formally requested the dotted line to sign on.

It took months to finalise. At Christmas, when schools were trying to book me to work with them the following term, I wrote to all my contacts, informing them I was leaving. The college was still not publicly confirming redundancies, so I thought it was more professional to say I was retiring and that my replacement hadn't been appointed yet. As I had no intention of seeking further paid employment (Mr C doesn't pay me), this wasn't actually untrue. I had some lovely farewell messages, saying the nicest things. I miss the friendships that developed from those working relationships, both in and outside of the college but I really love being able to say I'm retired, which I am!

Chapter Forty-Two

(23rd January 2016)

Attend the Adventure Travel Show

Marcia had given me a subscription to the Lonely Planet Magazine for Christmas the previous year and in one of the editions, they were offering half-priced tickets to the Adventure Travel Show at Olympia. It sounded amazing, offering inspiration for some very different types of holidays. Plus, it was a great opportunity for another weekend in London and a chance to see Josh (I was definitely suffering from Empty Nest Syndrome). I booked the tickets and some accommodation. We had ideas of places we'd like to visit and we definitely wanted to see what the Show had to offer with regard to diving holidays. Before we went, I did some costings for a diving holiday in the Maldives. We've never been but would love to go. I knew it could be expensive and started to correspond with a guy from a dive holiday specialist company, to see what our options were. Liking the idea of a week on a live-aboard dive boat followed by a week on an island, diving the house reef, he did us some costings. He was really helpful and gave us lots of options. He also pointed out that once you got there EVERYTHING is an extra, every soft drink, every beer, every dive … and none of them were cheap. In addition to the quote for the holiday I'd factored in spending money, so at least I had a ballpark total, should there be any offers at Olympia. We also wanted to find out about diving in Sipidan, an island off the coast of Borneo in the

Coral Triangle, renown for fantastic diving. Other than that, we were open to inspiration.

When we got there I was like a kid in a sweet shop, not knowing where to look first. It wasn't huge but there were plenty of exhibitors, so where to start? Looking at a map of the layout of the stands, we planned a route. Almost as soon as we started, we saw a stand about diving. A lovely young British couple, Simon and Sophie, had set off around the world looking for a place to set up a Dive Centre. They'd settled on an island called Bangka, just off the coast of North Sulawesi in Indonesia ... located in the Coral Triangle! We told them about our plans to re-visit Borneo in 2017, when we would be interested in diving at Sipidan. We were married in Borneo and always said we would return for our tenth wedding anniversary. They said the diving in Sipidan was still amazing but very restricted and that these days you needed permits, which were not always easy to come by and also that insurance is an issue, as there have been reported incidents of kidnapping. They explained that Bangka was in the same part of the ocean as Sipidan, with equally amazing marine life and showed us photos of the diving and their resort. Accommodation was very basic, with no hot water or air conditioning and outside bathrooms. One of their "rooms" was a bungalow on the beach. It looked awesome. We enquired about the cost and of a ten-day, twenty-seven-dive package, including bed and board, it was a fraction of the price of the Maldives and considerably cheaper to get to. Plus, the only extras would be beers and any additional diving. We explained that we had literally only just arrived at the show but took their literature, saying we were very interested and would probably be back with more questions later.

Continuing on I could have stopped at so many stalls but tried to remain focused … for our first circuit at least. We managed to pick up a few leaflets along the way, without getting too distracted, then as we rounded the corner there was a stand with an Enfield motorbike parked next to it. Mr C used to ride a lot but gave it up many years ago. I'd always enjoyed being a pillion when I lived in Somerset and Benefactor Bob had always had bikes, which I loved being on the back of but with my balance and coordination I'd never had any desire to ride one myself. We stopped to reminisce. A guy came over and we chatted about bikes in general, then he told us a bit about his company. Ken was CEO of Drifters, an adventure travel company in South Africa and was over to promote a new ten-day bike tour, following the diamond route from Cape Town to Kimberley.

I think I've expressed my passion for Africa already but I'd never been to South Africa. It was definitely on the "to do" list. Ken talked passionately and it sounded an incredible trip … probably with an incredible price tag. Before we could even ask, he said that the current exchange rate made it great value for money in the UK. When we did the conversion he was right and we were amazed. We took the leaflet about the tour and the brochure about the company and said we'd have a think about it. Dragging ourselves away, we continued our journey around the show. Somewhat surprisingly there weren't any other specific dive operators and nothing about the Maldives at all. We bumped into the guy who ran the company that we'd been to Morocco with, who'd also been our raft guide. We chatted to him for a bit but our minds were elsewhere.

"Fancy a coffee?" I said to Mr C. "Yep" he replied … and we both knew what we were thinking. We sat down with the leaflets, grinning at each other. We worked out that we could do both South Africa AND Bangka for pretty much the same price that we'd budgeted for two weeks in the Maldives. "What do you think?" I asked and with that we started seriously going through the possibilities. We decided that Simon and Sophie's offer was too good to miss. It was half the price of going to the Maldives and much more diving than we would do if we went to Sipidan. We made a list of things we wanted to ask them, like best time of year to visit, best way to get there and an idea of the cost of flights. Then we talked about the Enfield Tour and couldn't believe how excited we both were about the prospect of that. The leaflet listed the dates that the tour would be running, so we'd need to check our diaries to see if any of them worked for us, plus flight costs of course.

We went back to Simon and Sophie, got the information we needed and told them we'd check out flights when we got home but visiting them in October was a definite possibility. "Great" they said, "we'll make sure you get the bungalow on the beach". Then we went back to see Ken. We checked again that it wouldn't be a problem for us to do the tour on just one bike (it wouldn't) and if he had any suggestions regarding flights. He gave us a few pointers, which we duly noted, then as we were leaving, he said "Another nice thing to do is tack a safari on to the

Enfield Tour. You'll already have paid for your flights to get there and the exchange rate is so good". He showed us the relevant page in the brochure and smiled. We really liked the look of the Kruger Safari and the conversion did indeed make it very good value. What a salesman. We took his business card and said we'd be in touch.

We did book the diving holiday in Bangka, adding on a four day Discover Minahasa Tour in North Sulawesi at the end of our trip, which was described as the *"Perfect choice for first-timers to get to know Manado and Minahasa, the Land of Smiling People, with tours showcasing the local nature, wildlife, history, culture and people"*. After ten days exploring under the water it was a great way to sample the delights of above sea-level Indonesia. We also booked the epic Enfield Motorcycle Tour, adding on the five-day Kruger Safari at the beginning of our trip. All Bucket List adventures in themselves. As for the Adventure Travel Show? Suffice to say, it is a firm fixture on our calendar each year now.

Chapter Forty-Three
(23rd January 2016)

Take part in Fawlty Towers - The Dining Experience

This was a late entry, as it was a Christmas present from Mr C's brother Daran and our sister-in-law Kathrin but as we are both fans of Fawlty Towers and it's something completely different it had to be included. Luckily there was availability for the evening of the Adventure Travel Show, so it tied in nicely. Our Faulty Towers - The Dining Experience took place at the Amba Hotel in Charing Cross. Billed as a theatrical experience like no other that you actually get to play a part in, we had no idea what to expect.

When we arrived, we were shown to the bar which was a long, brightly lit room, already busy with our fellow diners. A short time later, there was a bit of a kerfuffle when "Basil" came in and started chatting to his "guests". Of course, he was rude to some and polite to others, as he circulated around the room. He scorned any late comers then, once everyone had arrived, called us forward by name to be seated. We sat at large round tables, in a very grand dining room, where Sybil and Manuel were welcoming and organising people. It really was like being an extra in an episode of the show itself, part-scripted and part-improvised. You never really knew what was going to happen next but Basil and Manuel did a lot of head-slamming, falling over and crockery smashing, as you'd expect.

We ate a 1970s style three course dinner but it wasn't really about the cuisine. The service was very random. Sometimes only one person on the table would get their food, plonked down in front of them by one of the characters, before they randomly wandered off to serve someone on another table. Sometimes, before you even started eating, they would whisk your meal away, giving it to someone else and leaving you with nothing. The first course was soup. Basil delivered mine and I was told it was very hot, so not to touch it until it cooled down. As people continued to be served, Basil suddenly shouted "Stop" and the room fell silent. He went on to explain that the chef had lost his false teeth! He asked if anyone had found them, so we all had a good old stir and to my amazement, they were in MY soup bowl. He came and fished them out, telling everyone to "carry on", before shouting "stop" once again, as he'd realised that the chef had two sets of dentures, top and bottom and one was still missing. There was even more hilarity when the second set turned up.

The evening carried on like that for two hours. I won't tell you too much about the "plot" in case you choose to get tickets for yourself (I believe these events take place regularly around the country). However, if you do go, be warned that those who were daring enough to excuse themselves for a comfort break received a tirade of abuse, both on the way out and on the way back in again. In fact, one poor chap wasn't allowed to go at all. So, make sure you go before you go! It's definitely a laugh-out-loud experience all the way through and very cleverly done. What a great Christmas present, lucky us.

Chapters Forty-Four & Forty-Five

(16th – 17th February 2016)

Visit Pompeii

&

Visit Vesuvius

For a bit of culture, I needed to put these two iconic places on my List. I remember being fascinated by both Pompeii and Vesuvius as a child, after watching an episode of Blue Peter (strange the things you remember) and promised, one day, I'd see it for myself. Over the last few years we've tried to take an annual mini break to a European city with Keith and Sara. So far, we'd been to Krakow, Budapest and Prague. This year we chose Naples.

After another early start from the UK, by 11am we were checked-in to our hotel and off exploring. We could see Vesuvius across the bay but had planned to spend the first day getting our bearings and wandering around Naples. When I think of cities in Italy, it conjures up images of grand architecture, with neat streets full of very stylish, chic Italians. I assumed this was how Naples would be, with Capri just across the water and UNESCO World Heritage Sites on the doorstep. Sadly, our first impression wasn't the best because although it has some lovely buildings and some really nice parts, a lot of the city was run down and dirty. I've never seen so much rubbish on the streets and there was graffiti everywhere. Nonetheless, our hotel was nice and it was a great location for the places we wanted to visit.

Orientation complete, we did the usual thing, consulting guidebooks and picking up leaflets to plan the best itinerary that would enable us to see as much as possible during our short stay. Pompeii was first on the list. We took a bus to the station, then boarded a train. The graffiti was incredible, both on the trains and the platforms. At some of the stops we couldn't even read the station name as the signs had been completely covered. Luckily our stop was pretty obvious and it was just a short walk to the entrance of Pompeii. Although it was February, the weather was sunny and warm as we meandered down the cobbled streets. The city was so much bigger than we'd imagined and we spent over five hours there, immersed in the history. Although we didn't have a guide, we think we managed to see pretty much everything. It wasn't hard to imagine what life would have been like in those ancient times and the fear the inhabitants must have experienced when the volcano, clearly visible to the city's populace, erupted.

The following day, we headed to Vesuvius. Disembarking from the train (the same one that takes you to Pompeii, so we knew the routine), we queued to purchase tickets for the shuttle bus, which takes you part of the way. It was early and there appeared to be some confusion as to when the shuttle service would actually start, so we found a café close by where we could watch what was going on and not miss our slot. Mr C and I ordered white coffees, at least we thought that was what we'd ordered. What we were actually served was two glasses of hot milk, followed by two shots of coffee, the confusion obviously coming from us asking for "coffee with milk", which is what, quite literally, the waiter gave us. So, we made our DIY milky coffees and continued to monitor the transport situation. Shuttle buses started arriving and people started gathering, so we finished our drinks and joined the crowd, although there was no obvious place to queue (how British are we). It was all pretty disorganised and people were getting on buses ad hoc, so we decided to dispense with being polite and just jump on the next available one.

It was a scenic ride up to the National Park, where we were dropped off to continue the ascent on foot, with spectacular views across the bay. Arriving at the ticket office for the summit, we were informed that being part of a guided group was compulsory, so we waited with a collection of English-speaking people until we were summoned. Our guide took us on a tour up to and partway around the rim of the crater. Seeing the volcano in its current dormant state, it's almost impossible to imagine the devastation it has caused during its life. Of course, there were signs of activity and one day there will be another eruption, although seeing it as it is now, that seems hard to comprehend. Once again, the panorama was spectacular and it was incredible to be standing on the top of this ancient beast.

As we looked out across the landscape, we were surprised that Pompeii was further away than we'd expected. Before our visit, we'd envisaged it nestling in the foothills of the volcano but in reality, it was some considerable distance away, making the enormity of the impact on that stricken city all the more sobering. Also, not far below us was Herculaneum which, although less known, had suffered a similar fate to Pompeii and that was where we were off to next.

The descent from Vesuvius was much quicker, both on foot and by bus and by midday we were in the ruins of Herculaneum. Somewhat surprisingly, there were very few visitors and as we purchased our tickets, an official gentleman offered to be our guide. We decided this would be a good idea, as we had a few unanswered questions from our visit to Pompeii, although we'd made up some pretty good stories about how we thought it all would have been, so some clarification would be good. This turned out to be a great decision. As he walked us around this former port, which was originally considerably closer to the sea, he brought everything to life, with stories of its inhabitants and what became of them. It really was like stepping back in time. Our explorations of this area had certainly given us a much greater insight into this chapter of its history.

While staying in Naples, we'd hoped to visit Capri, which is relatively close and clearly visible in the bay. However, we were told that, at this time of year, nothing on the island would be open. So, for our last full day, we decided we'd visit the Amalfi Coast instead. Earlier in the weekend we'd used a taxi, which was absolutely immaculate and spotlessly clean. Hanging on the back of the driver's seat was a leaflet, saying it was available for private hire to do a variety of tours, including the

Amalfi Coast. Included was a list of prices, so out of interest we'd picked one up. Although he didn't speak much English, we'd also taken the taxi driver's name and number, saying we may be interested in hiring him. Trying to plan the visit by public transport had proved to be a bit of a logistical nightmare but between four of us, the taxi was a reasonable price and would give us the freedom to stop and go as we pleased, so the choice was obvious. Once we'd decided that's what we wanted to do, we asked the hotel staff to call our driver, as we knew language would be a problem, to explain what we would like to do and to arrange a pickup time. All sorted ... or so we thought.

The next morning, we were met by Francesco, the taxi driver's son, in a completely different but much bigger (and equally spotless) vehicle. He explained that his English was better than his Dad's, so he'd been asked to take his place. He questioned us about what we wanted to see along the Amalfi Coast and decided the best route for us would be to start at Ravello and drive back along the coast to Sorrento, for a nice meal before returning to the hotel. It sounded ideal. It took us about an hour to reach Ravello, passing Vesuvius and Pompeii, heading south to a pass with lots of switchbacks, as we climbed up and over the mountain range.

When we got to the coast, the scenery was breath-taking. The winding road was very narrow, climbing high as it clung precariously to the cliff edge, occasionally dipping steeply down into pretty little towns and villages along the way. Being out of season, the roads and towns were really quiet and although it would have been nice to see them in the summer sun, being able to wander around without the crowds was a delight. Apparently, in the height of the season they operate a one-way route along the coast because there are so many tourists and we've subsequently heard from friends, who have visited during the summer, that driving when it's that busy is absolutely terrifying. After Ravello, Francesco took us to Amalfi and Positano, stopping at spectacular viewpoints along the way and never rushing us to leave, as we soaked in the beauty of the dramatic scenery. What better way to visit this exquisite part of our world? We'd definitely made the right decision.

From Positano we cut across to Sorrento. Francesco asked what sort of thing we'd like to eat, then said he knew just the place. He took us to Ristorante Tasso which, to be honest, looked a bit posh. He seemed to know the staff there and we started to wonder if he was on commission and we'd been a little bit gullible. We couldn't have been more wrong. The food was absolutely superb. It looked amazing, tasted amazing and was really good value for money. We were replete!

Arriving back in Naples by late afternoon, we had just enough time to squeeze in a guided tour of Napoli Sotterranea, an Ancient Greek-Roman aqueduct, forty metres below ground. The labyrinth of waterways, passages and cisterns takes you on a fascinating journey through nearly two-and-a-half thousand years of history.

Emerging after a couple of hours beneath the bustling streets of the city, we found ourselves in need of some authentic refreshment. Even though it was now evening, we wanted to be outside and in the Piazza San Domenico Maggiore we found the San Domenico Café. Keith and Sara recommended the Aperol Spritz Ritual. Aperol is a digestive and the ritual, born in Veneto, claims to be the quintessential aperitif. Equal parts of Prosecco and Aperol are poured over ice, with a splash of soda, topped with a slice of orange. The Aperol Spritz is then served with some traditional snacks called "cicchetti", small dishes that usually include tiny sandwiches, plates of olives and petite portions of local dishes. It was a great way to sit and reflect on all that we'd managed to cram into our mini break.

Chapter Forty-Six

(9th March 2016)

Visit the Sky Garden

This one was a recommendation from Dot, a good friend who had also been Head of Schools Liaison many moons ago. Coincidentally, our paths should have crossed years before we met at work, as her husband, Peter, knew Steve when they served in the Submarine Service together. I love the way fate sometimes gives you a second chance to reconnect. It's funny really, I've always said that I don't generally socialise with people I work with, at least not when we're actually working together, preferring to keep business and pleasure separate but when I look back, I've formed strong and lasting friendships with lots of people from work over the years. Josh always loved Dot. Whenever he came into the office with me, she would have a packet of chocolate buttons waiting for him. It became their special "thing". She even gave him a packet when he went off to University! When Dot left college to move to North Wales, we kept in touch and visited on numerous occasions. Although her girls were older, he idolised them and would drag them down to the bridge at the end of the road to play Pooh Sticks in the stream … as many times as he could get away with.

When Dot turned fifty, she wanted a Ceilidh to celebrate. Josh, Mr C and I were all invited, as were Keith and Sara. You see, we'd all worked together at the college at one point. Keith was one of the first people I'd met when I started. He was a lecturer and also seconded to Schools

Liaison, one day a week, during term time. When Dot was leading Schools Liaison, Sara came to work in the Marketing Department, as part of her degree. She subsequently returned to the college, once she'd graduated and lead the Schools Liaison team, after Dot left. So, we all go back quite a long way.

It made sense to drive up together on the Friday night and share accommodation, which was a little holiday cottage, just outside the village where the Ceilidh would take place. As quite a few people were travelling and arriving the night before, Dot had arranged an informal gathering in the village pub. Towards the end of the evening, Peter took me to one side and said, "You haven't arranged anything for Dot's birthday, have you?" and gave me a bit of a wink. This may have been because we'd done all sorts of things for her fortieth birthday, which, for some reason, I had been held responsible for. With a smile I assured him that I hadn't … because I really hadn't and he gave me a hug and walked off. I didn't think much more of it until I was relaying the story to Keith and Sara back at the cottage over a bottle of wine. Then I started to question it. Did he mean "You haven't arranged anything for Dot's birthday have you (I hope you have)?" or did he mean "You haven't arranged anything for Dot's birthday have you (don't you dare)?". After another bottle of wine (or two) and much discussion, we decided he MUST have meant "I hope you have" but what on earth could we plan with less than twenty-four hours' notice and in a part of the country we didn't know very well?

We started brainstorming. A strip-a-gram was out of the question, even if there was such a thing these days. She didn't enjoy the one who turned up for her fortieth! So, what did she like? Well, she'd always liked chickens. We'd bought her lots of chickens over the years. In fact, I think she had a rubber one for her fortieth ... oops! Surely, in these rural parts, we'd find something to do with chickens ... and then the plan was "hatched". We were up early in the morning, to start putting the idea into action. First, we spoke to the lady who owned the cottage. "Do you know anywhere we can get a chicken?" we asked. "What sort of chicken?" she enquired. "A real one" was the reply. Unfazed, as if it was the sort of thing she got asked all the time by guests, she put her thinking cap on.

She didn't know of any farms locally that could help but there was a place, nearby, that had all sorts of rescue animals. She told us where it was and gave us their number. "One more thing" I said, "If we do manage to get a chicken, are you OK with us bringing it back to the cottage? It's only until this evening". We knew animals were allowed because in the kitchen were some dog bowls for people to use (for their dogs obviously, not as human crockery!). "Of course," she replied, again as if people bought chickens on holiday all the time. With bated breath we called the rescue place. "Do you have any chickens?" I asked. "We've got a few but they're pretty old and don't lay anymore" was the response. "That's not a problem. Would you be prepared to re-home one?" I asked tentatively. "I don't see why not" he said and we made arrangements to meet later in the day. Great, we had a chicken, now we had to find something to put it in. What could be more appropriate than a basket? Everyone loves chicken in a basket!

We found a pet shop and bought the cutest wicker cat basket, then set off to the rescue centre. When we arrived, the man took us to a pen containing a few hens and a cockerel and told us to take our pick. He did look at us a little strangely when we produced the cat basket, lined with newspaper, to put her in but luckily, didn't ask too many questions. "I'll put some feed in a bag for you to be going on with" he said kindly. We asked him how much he wanted for her and he said he didn't sell animals but would happily accept a donation towards their food. So, we gave him a few pounds and off we went. Sorted! Accept it was only mid-day. The party wasn't until the evening and we'd planned to go for a bit of a walk in Snowdonia. No problem, KFC (that's what we'd called her) could come too. We were only going for a short walk, so she'd be fine in the car. Josh carried her on his lap, in the back of the car, for the short journey to the National Park but we were a bit concerned about leaving her in full view while we were away. What if someone stole her (because of course that was highly likely)? We decided to put her in the boot, out of sight. Bertha had a huge boot and we weren't going to be that long, so she'd be quite alright. We'd leave some food for her and because it would be dark, she'd probably sleep. Safely hidden, we set off for a quick bimble. When we got back to the car, she was absolutely fine and (I like to think) pleased to see us.

Returning to the cottage, it seemed a shame to keep her cooped up in her basket because she was going to have to spend the rest of the evening in there at the Ceilidh, so we set her on the floor and opened the door so she could wander out. It was a bit unusual seeing a chicken wandering around a lounge but she seemed quite at home. She was very friendly and not scared of us at all. In fact, she took great delight in jumping up to sit on Keith's lap. Unfortunately, Keith isn't that fond of birds and looked quite ill-at-ease as she eyed him this way and that. Next, we had to think about how we were going to get her to the Ceilidh. Dot had booked a minibus to come and pick up everyone staying at the cottages. Should we just be upfront and ask the driver if it was OK to bring a chicken on board? What if he said "No"? We'd be scuppered then. We decided it was probably best to smuggle her on board and hope that nobody asked any questions.

Then we had to decide how to "gift wrap" her? We fetched the picnic blanket from the car and draped it over the basket, with a makeshift bow on top. Perfect. When the transport arrived, we gave her to Josh to carry, thinking he was the least likely to be challenged and luckily, the driver didn't bat an eyelid. Arriving at the village hall, we put her on a table in the foyer, away from the loud music. We went in to find Dot and Peter. "Come with us" we said, "we've got you a present" and Peter looked at me quizzically. Cautiously, Dot lifted the edge of the blanket. "It's a chicken!" she exclaimed. We all grinned and nodded. "A real chicken!" she said. We nodded again. "She's called KFC" we said proudly "Happy Birthday!". Peter looked in the basket and shook his head. I smiled and shrugged my shoulders. "When you said, "You haven't arranged anything for Dot's birthday have you?" I knew you really meant you wanted us to do something, so we have!" I assured him. "No" he said, "what I meant was - don't you dare!" but he was smiling when he said it. Explaining how friendly she was, we took her out for Dot to cuddle. We have some great photos, with Dot looking about as comfortable as Keith did as she held her (KFC ... not Dot). She was the star of the evening, KFC that is ... although Dot did share the limelight with her! When we checked out of the cottage the following day, the lady asked, "Did you get your chicken?" ... just another average day in North Wales then!

So, as I was saying, the Sky Garden was something Dot recommended. Located in London, at 20 Fenchurch Street, it is described as; *a unique public space that spans three storeys and offers three hundred-and-sixty-degree uninterrupted views across the City of London. Visitors can wander around the exquisitely landscaped gardens, observation decks and an open-air terrace of what is London's highest public garden.*

I'd started occasionally taking the coach to London for the day, getting to spend some QFT with Josh and I thought this would be a nice treat for both of us. You have to pre-book a specific entry time but once you're there, you can stay as long as you like. It's a really lovely space and we whiled away a couple of hours, looking at the views, drinking coffee, sitting in the gardens and just generally catching up. Special times in a beautiful setting. Great recommendation Dot, sorry about the chicken!

Chapter Forty-Seven

(14th March 2016)

Celebrate Dad's 90th Birthday

This is a very special entry and one I hadn't dared put on the List when I started it. My Dad was a bit of a medical miracle. He'd always been a very fit and active man, eating healthily and although not a sportsman, taking regular exercise and doing lots of walking (and indeed swimming when they had their pool in Spain). Working in the building trade was physically demanding too. His health was generally good but whenever he did have a blip, it would be a big one. Diagnosed with angina, at the age of sixty-six he needed a quadruple heart bypass, which his consultant said should give him a good ten to fifteen years. Mum and Dad were living in Spain at the time but had a base in the UK (the house just down the road from Debbi and Morgan), which they returned to for his operation. He recovered well and they were soon back in the sunshine on the Costa de la Luz. Some years later, he was rushed to hospital in Cadiz, suffering from heart problems. While he was in the observation ward he suffered a massive heart attack which, if he hadn't been where he was at the time, would have finished him off. The medical care and attention he received was fantastic, probably due to the fact that he was in a state-of-the-art teaching hospital. I flew out to be with Mum and it was a tense few weeks. I can't praise the staff enough for their patience and consideration. Every couple of days we would be called in for a meeting with a consultant, who would update us on his progress (Dad's, not the consultant's). The trouble was, although Mum spoke quite good conversational Spanish, when it came to medical matters we were way out of our depth. Luckily, we had friends locally who could help. Ann and Andy lived on the same golf course as Mum and Dad. She was American and he was Spanish. Although they knew a little of each other's languages, as they'd met in Germany they would talk to each other predominantly in German. We'd take them with us when the doctors had something particularly important to say, explaining things to Andy in Spanish, who would translate it into German for Ann, who would translate it into English for us! It was a bit long-winded but it worked.

Dad improved and was moved to a medical ward where I would sometimes stay overnight, in a chair by his bed, because that's what families do over there. With the medical insurance they had, once he was deemed well enough to fly, he was brought back to the UK, escorted by a doctor who monitored him throughout the flight. In time, he made a good recovery. After much soul-searching, Mum and Dad decided it wasn't practical living in Spain anymore, with the responsibilities of a large villa and an enormous garden. They started bringing some of their belongings back to the UK, then in October 1996 the villa was sold and they were ready to come home. I'd just finished my temporary contract at the college (you may remember), so Steve and I took Dad's estate car, that he kept in the UK, on the ferry to Bilbao, then drove down to Cadiz. Using both the estate and the saloon car that they had in Spain, we loaded up the last of their possessions and drove in convoy, back through Spain and France, all the way home.

It was a hilarious journey because every inch of both cars had something wedged in it, leaving just enough room for the driver. Also, just before we left, Mum and I had popped over to Gibraltar, which we always did, where I'd slipped and twisted my ankle. It was nothing serious but it swelled up like a balloon and was a bit stiff. Luckily, it was my left ankle and we were going to be on motorways most of the time, so I wouldn't have to use the clutch too often. Also, I was five months pregnant but that's a minor detail.

The roads were good and relatively traffic free. To make our journey as quick as possible we used the toll roads but in a right-hand drive car which is packed to the gunnels, when we got to the toll booths, we had to get out of the cars and walk around to pay. On top of that because I hadn't used the clutch for a while, my ankle would stiffen up, so when I did get out and walk I was hobbling. I must have looked a right sight. At our first fuel stop I pulled up at pump number fourteen. Unfortunately, when I went in to pay, try as I might I just couldn't remember the Spanish word for fourteen. I knew how to say "one" and "four" but that only added to the confusion, when the cashier thought I was paying for two pumps. We sorted it out eventually.

Fortunately, when the ferry docked at Portsmouth the customs men waved us straight through. Just as well, as it would have taken forever to unload that lot if they wanted to search us. I think they took one look and thought better of it. Mum and Dad flew home and settled in a flat on the seafront not far from us. It all worked out for the best in the end because it meant they were around when Josh was born and have played a hugely important part in his life growing up, which has given them all a lot of enjoyment and created a very special bond.

We had a fantastic surprise seventieth birthday for Dad, in the Senior Rates Mess on HMS Victory. We quite literally pushed the boat out and had a good old knees-up. For his eightieth we had a family party at our house because to be honest, nothing could top his seventieth. Nobody could ever believe how old he was because he always looked so good. Even doctors and nurses would question his age, particularly when they saw his medical records.

A few years ago, Mum and Dad decided they wanted to move to something with a garden and started looking around at properties for sale. They considered buying a run-down old bungalow, which needed complete renovation and talked about living in a caravan in the garden while they did it up! Well, they'd done it before! However, we reminded them that was forty-plus years ago, when they were just a tad younger. Luckily, we talked them out of that one. Fortunately, nobody had made a decent offer for their flat. I say fortunately because Dad's health began to decline and they realised that a move was now totally impractical. The flat was manageable and the sea views were great, so although they'd had a lot of fun doing the research, they made the sensible decision to stay put.

I can't really pinpoint exactly when Dad started to slow down. We didn't really realise how ill he was until our trip to Skern Lodge, to celebrate my fiftieth and Josh's eighteenth. He was very wobbly on his feet, sleeping a lot and just not well enough to have even made the journey, let alone the weekend. Mum didn't want to leave him but was desperate to come and Dad wanted her to go too. So, we employed a live-in carer for the weekend, just to keep an eye on things.

Shortly after that, Dad took a turn for the worse and Mum had to call an ambulance. As an insulin dependent diabetic, he'd hypoed in the night. Mum couldn't get his blood sugars up and he was delirious. The paramedics couldn't sort him out either so, at 4am, Mr C and I followed them in the ambulance and he was admitted to hospital. He was very frail and weak but when each doctor came to look at him, asking how he was, he would reply, as always, "I'm fine".

He wasn't fine though, he was very poorly indeed. It was touch and go for a couple of weeks but they managed to stabilise him and put together a care package, enabling him to come home. That was at the end of May 2015. From then on he had carers coming in four times a day to help with his personal care and medication and was closely monitored by Lisa, a specialist heart failure nurse, who visited regularly. She was amazing, a great support to all of us (and we've now become friends outside of work).

Seeing just how unwell he had been, we really didn't think we'd get to celebrate his ninetieth birthday but Dad being Dad, thankfully defied the odds and made it. We had a small family gathering at ours on the Sunday before his birthday. Being pretty much housebound, getting him over to our house was exhausting for him but he was a determined old what-not and once he was settled he thoroughly enjoyed his day out.

I wanted to do something to make his actual birthday special but it's really difficult to think of something for someone at his stage of life. Having one of my lightbulb moments, I decided to use the thing we all have at our fingertips, social media and put this message out on Facebook;

On a bit of a mission today! For those that don't know, my Dad is going to be 90 on 14th March 2016. There is nothing he wants or needs but as the Queen doesn't do telegrams for 90-year-olds, I thought it might be nice to fill his home with as many cards as possible. So, if you'd like to send him one, message me and I will give you his address. Thank you. x

I was overwhelmed by the response. He had so many cards to open it looked more like Christmas and the good thing was, it gave Mum and Dad something to talk about for days, trying to work out who everybody was and finding out about the lovely people who had sent their best wishes despite being complete strangers. My heartfelt thanks to everyone who made this possible.

It is with pride and admiration that I include this milestone on my Bucket List. A very special entry for a very special man. I love you Dad xxx

Chapter Forty-Eight

Make a personalised blanket

As I mentioned back in Chapter Twenty-One, after the conception of Ruby, in a traffic jam in France, I'd started planning a crocheted blanket for her. By now you know that I am always a starter and never a finisher, so you won't be surprised that I started making some big granny squares for my throw. Unfortunately, I'm not that good at crochet, so it made very slow progress and surprise, surprise ... I didn't get around to finishing it.

As luck would have it, sometime later, Kath's Mum and Dad were downsizing. Kath went up to Barnsley to help them pack and while they were sorting through everything, came across a blanket that her sister Mel had crocheted as a teenager. Having no use for it anymore, it was allocated to the charity pile. "If you don't want that I'll take it for Lesley" Kath grinned. She checked with Mel, to make sure she didn't want it for herself. "What, that old thing? She's welcome to it" was her response.

I was delighted when Kath gave it to me, it was just what I wanted and very genuinely retro. It took pride of place in the back of Ruby ... and my efforts got "shelved". From time to time, Jo asked how my squares were coming along (well you can never have too many crocheted blankets). I confessed that I'd lost the enthusiasm now that I had the one Mel made but I kept the ones I'd made so far and would look at them from time to time, hoping to finish it one day, having invested quite a bit of time and effort in it over the years.

My Birthday Bucket List gave me the opportunity to finish it, as a keepsake for my memorable year. Enlisting the help of friends, I asked if anyone would be interested in making me a woollen square. It could be knitted or crocheted, in any colour, the only thing that was fixed were the dimensions. I've got some very lovely, very talented friends and over the year, built up a collection of squares in various colours and patterns. I crocheted a couple more granny squares myself, to complete the patchwork effect I was looking for, alternating one of my squares with one of theirs on each row. I stitched them all together and crocheted a border.

I am pleased to announce that, for once, I am a finisher and I am now the very proud owner of a beautiful, colourful, blanket with a very special meaning.

Chapter Forty-Nine

Complete a project with crocheted flowers

Like the woollen squares, I didn't want everything on my List to be big and extravagant. As well as having adventures and making memories, I wanted to create some sentimental keepsakes. When Jo visits her sister in Pembrokeshire, not that far from Rob and Jo, she often returns with some wonderfully creative ideas. She'd shown me some photos she'd taken of a beautiful chair which had been reupholstered, then embellished with a swathe of hundreds of different crocheted flowers. It looked amazing but I knew it would take me a lifetime to make that many blooms. Time to enlist my friends again I think, although the only truly accomplished crocheter amongst us is Jo herself. Still, you've got to start somewhere, so we decided that one of our Pink Ladies get-togethers should be a crochet tutorial evening.

We had plenty of hooks and wool between us and Jo arrived armed with patterns. I plied the girls with bubbles and nibbles and the fun began. After the usual animated chit chat, catching up on each other's news (we don't all get together like this that often), we settled down to the main event. At this stage, I would like to point out that we were a very mixed ability group. Whilst some of us had made some crocheted things in the past, some had never even picked up a crochet hook but we were doing this as a team, so we all started together at square (or should I say flower) one. Jo started with how to hold the hook and the wool, then demonstrated how to make a basic chain. The level of concentration was incredible and the sense of achievement at being able to produce a long, neat set of stitches was cosmic.

Once she was happy that the fundamental principles had been mastered there were gasps and giggles as she showed us how to make a simple flower. By now, we were all up for it in a big way. Everyone was engrossed as they embarked on their maiden blossoms. When the Pink Ladies normally get together, the volume is colossal but now, with everyone so focused, you could hear a pin drop. From time to time there were groans of frustration but Jo would calmly step in to get things back on track. The excitement when each flower was complete was astounding and once we'd got the hang of it, we all wanted to make more. Creations came thick and fast, well not that fast but you know what I mean. It was like being in the workshop of a woollen florist's.

Levels of success were, to be honest, varied but each was a recognisable flower. As confidence grew, so did the different designs and at one-point Kath was even free-styling, making it up as she went along. By the end of the evening, everybody was very proud of their endeavours. Most of the flowers made that night formed the foundation of my final collection but a few were taken home for "show and tell" (I imagine their husbands were thrilled). Of course, we didn't make enough to cover a chair but it was a start and over the months that followed, I enlisted the help of anyone (or their friends and family) who was prepared to add to the compendium and my stockpile increased.

It became obvious that the quantity required for a chair was far in excess of what I had, so I decided to downsize my project to a footstool. I found an unwanted old fashioned one, removed the fringing from around the edge and began attaching my floral extravaganza. It now sits in pride of place in the conservatory, where it is used regularly and is a constant reminder to the girls of their sterling efforts when they visit.

Chapter Fifty

Write a book about my 50th Birthday Bucket List

So, this is it! The Book. The last chapter, in more ways than one, as this was always going to be the final challenge. Sadly not completed within the year but realistically, I never thought that was possible. On 13th April 2016 I removed the paper copy of my Bucket List from the wall (with all but this one challenge ticked off), popped it in my hand luggage and set off for Lanzarote. Armed with my laptop, my diary, all my photos and a head full of ideas, I started writing this book. I thought writing up my adventures was going to be the most difficult task to date but once I got going, I couldn't stop. Travelling alone meant I could do what I wanted, when I wanted and with no other agenda I could write for hours on end. My body clock was completely out of whack though, finding it easier to write at night because the distraction of blue skies and sunshine during the day proved too much. So I became pretty nocturnal, sleeping on a sunbed during the day then burning the midnight oil, slaving away over my laptop at night. Sometimes I would collapse into bed, exhausted, in the early hours but my brain wouldn't switch off, I was so engrossed. I always tried to complete the chapter I was working on before I closed my laptop down for the night but in preparation for my next shift I would type the title of the following chapter, ready for the off. The trouble with doing this is that I would lay there, willing myself to sleep, trying to make my mind blank but mulling over the next instalment. Try as I might I couldn't switch off. I would make mental notes about things I wanted to say, then I'd come up with (what I thought was) a really good phrase. Worried that I'd have forgotten it by the morning, I would get up, power up my laptop and type it in.

Of course, then I'd be back on the hamster wheel, as one thing would lead to another and suddenly, I'd be working on that chapter, pushing myself to get it finished while I was in full flow. Sometimes I was getting up two or three times a night, hence sleeping on the beach or by the pool during the day was essential.

When I started, my writing was so prolific that I convinced myself that I'd get it cracked in a week … yeah right! As the end of my trip loomed, I had to accept that, although I was pleased with the work I'd done so far, it was nowhere near completion. However, I calculated that if, when I got home, I set aside just an hour a night, I could have it finished within a couple of months. The trouble is, neither life nor I work like that. It sounds a good plan but what can you actually achieve in an hour? By the time you've set yourself up, got back on track from where you left off and thought about what you are going to write your hour is pretty much accounted for. Coupled with that, at home there are just too many other distractions. There would always be chores to do, or Mr C "trying" to be quiet, which usually meant talking to himself (or very loudly on the phone to someone else), singing along with the radio or laughing at something he was watching on TV (because if I was writing, he'd take the opportunity to watch the rubbish that he finds hilarious but I can't stand). The situation was not ideal and my creative juices just stopped flowing. I realised the only time I could write was when I had solitude and in our busy lives, there wasn't a lot of that around. So, although I didn't plan it this way, it turned out that the only time I could ever make any progress was when I was away on my own, which is my excuse for why finishing my book has taken so long.

The next time I added any text was May 2017 and the time after that was … now … May 2018. So, when you look at it like that, it has only really taken me three weeks (in Lanzarote) to write this book, quite a feat after all. For the record, the final edits were not complete until 2019 (in Jamaica) but I don't want to muddy the waters with such minor details. I've actually surprised myself at how much I've enjoyed the whole process, although that might have something to do with the locations. As I said right at the beginning, this book has been written predominantly for myself and therefore I think I've achieved what I set out to do. I know I've waffled on a bit (OK … a lot) in places and sometimes the back stories are far longer than the actual story about that particular challenge but that's me and after all, it is all about me. I'm glad that I've done this for Josh too, perhaps as something he can look back on and maybe share with his children when I'm not around to tell the tales myself anymore.

If anybody else wants to read it, that's great but if they don't, then that's OK too. I guess that was a pretty useless sentence actually because if you've got this far you've obviously chosen to read it (unless you're one of those people that reads the end of a book first, decides it's rubbish and bins it straight away). Many friends have expressed an interest in my completed project, especially those that feature in these pages. I hope they are satisfied with the way they have been portrayed and don't judge me too much for my accuracies (or inaccuracies). To the best of my knowledge, as much as a fifty-plus-year-old brain will allow, all that I have written is true. Would I do it again? Maybe. I still have a lot of stories to tell, so I'm sure I could begin if I wanted to but the completion of volume two would be uncertain. As I've stated throughout, I'm a starter not a finisher … only in this case, I've proved myself wrong.

So, in closing, my hope is that this may have inspired you to have adventures of your own. Life is out there for the taking and my advice to everybody is to take it while you can.

(hopefully not) THE END

With special thanks to my husband, my son, my wonderful friends and family (without whom, none of this would have been possible), Indie Foulkes for designing my front cover and Fontware for providing my barcode. I love you all x